A School at Shrewsbury

THE FOUR FOUNDATIONS

A School at Shrewsbury

THE FOUR FOUNDATIONS

Colin Leach

JAMES & JAMES

DESIGN
Caroline Archer

PHOTOGRAPHY
David Houlston

British Library Cataloguing in Publication Data
Leach, J. H. C. (J H Colin)
A school at Shrewsbury: the four foundations.
1. England. Schools, history
I. Title
371.00942

ISBN 0907383 06 8

First published 1990

TYPESETTING
Columns of Reading

PRINTED
in Great Britain, by BAS Printers Limited
at Over Wallop, Hampshire

PUBLISHED
by James and James
75 Carleton Rd
London N70ET

Title page picture: Shrewsbury School – the chapel, main school building and School House, from a 1977 drawing by John Western.

FOREWORD

by Sir Godfray Le Quesne
President Old Salopian Club

'Shrewsbury had entered into me; I loved every stone of it.' I have shared that experience of R. A. Knox, and can testify, like him, to my 'affection for the place, and the life of the place, and the friends I made there'.

Yet I had very imperfect knowledge of the school I thought I knew so well. This I realize, as many Salopians will, after reading Mr. Leach's book. He tells with consummate skill the whole dramatic story of Shrewsbury's beginning and growth and decline and rebirth, nor does he stop short of its modern transformation.

The school has been very fortunate in its settings, first the fine old buildings in the town, then the much finer position on Kingsland, above (in Knox's words again) 'the adorable curve of the Severn that flows under the schools'. It has been still more fortunate in the remarkable succession of men under whose influence generations of Salopians have passed. Some of them each of us has known in his own time. Mr. Leach portrays the most prominent of every epoch, from Thomas Ashton to the present day. He has given new light and new fascination to a notable and continuing story.

Non tacendumst hic priorum
Nobilem cohortem.

. . .

Floreat Salopia.

CONTENTS

LIST OF COLOUR PLATES

ACKNOWLEDGMENTS

I am very grateful to the Governing Body of the School for giving me the opportunity to write this book.

The book was started with most helpful encouragement from Simon Langdale, still then the Headmaster. In preparing it, I have received nothing but courtesy, help, and goodwill, and have had the good fortune to talk with Headmasters and masters past and present. I am happy to take this opportunity of warmly thanking Donald Wright, Eric Anderson, Ted Maidment, Derek Crompton, Stacy Colman (once my long-suffering form-master), Richard Raven, Peter Hughes, David Gee, Alan Laurie, Richard Brain, and James Lawson, the Schools' devoted and learned archivist and librarian. A new boy, Gabriel Cheng, courteously showed me over the new boarding House, The Grove. I leave to last the man to whom my greatest debt is owed: no Salopian will be surprised to hear that I mean Michael Charlesworth. His name does not appear among the list of Headmasters, though he has been acting Headmaster on three separate occasions (and was once seconded to be Headmaster of a public school in Pakistan, which now regularly seeks his return). He has been Housemaster of School House, a formidable task. He has acted as bursar on two separate occasions. He has been President of the Old Salopian Club. He edited the splendid and essential *Newsletter* for a quarter of a century. He has played in two winning Arthur Dunn Cup teams. In what may laughingly be referred to as his 'retirement', close to the Schools, he is producing an updated edition of the Salopian *Register*. It was said that, in his absence, seven people were needed to carry out his duties. For very many Old Salopians, he epitomizes Shrewsbury, and if this book were to be dedicated to only one man, he would be that man.

Finally, it is a pleasure to acknowledge the practical help that I received from Catheryn Kilgarriff and Kate Harris at James and James; and to thank Liz Ryder for her superlative typing.

Colin Leach
April 1990

TO ALL THOSE WHO TAUGHT ME
AT SHREWSBURY SCHOOL

When Edward the Sixth was a stripling
And Warwick believed him a fool,
The Severn went placidly rippling
Past Shrewsbury, lacking a school:
But Edward exclaimed, 'By our garter,
We'll alter this scandal ere long!'
So he drew up a grand Royal Charter
And set the boys singing this song:
'Floreat Salopia!'

D. F. T. COKE

1

PREFATORY NOTE

IT IS a rare school that can make and justify the claim to have been founded on no fewer than four occasions. Of course, the official date of the foundation of Shrewsbury School – as of some forty others – was 1552, in the brief reign of Edward VI, and, more relevantly, soon after the dissolution of the monasteries. But this first foundation seems not quite to have 'taken', and the history of the school really begins with the headmastership, under new ordinances, of Thomas Ashton, beginning in 1561; now began Shrewsbury's first period of real distinction, a period which, nevertheless, was followed in the eighteenth century by one of such decline that, as will be seen in due course, the school came close to extinction. Rescued at its third 'foundation' – again under new ordinances – by Samuel Butler in 1798, Shrewsbury enjoyed throughout the nineteenth century such success that Butler was able convincingly to argue as early as 1820 for its addition to the six public schools of a proposed Parliamentary Bill; and it was later duly included among the schools listed in the Public Schools Act of 1868. Yet even then it became apparent that pressing problems loomed; and the school's fourth 'foundation' can be said to have occurred when, by an act of supreme foresight, Henry Whitehead Moss successfully procured its removal in 1882 from its picturesque but desperately cramped buildings in the centre of the town to the outstanding site at Kingsland which it now occupies. There has happily been no need for a fifth foundation as, in the past century, Shrewsbury has consolidated and built upon its success.

The historians of that long success have not been few: the unfinished Blakeway *History* of 1889, G. W. Fisher's *Annals of Shrewsbury School* (1899), and J. B. Oldham's *History* (1952) are outstanding, but are far from alone. Philip Cowburn's *A Salopian Anthology* (1964) deserves mention; memoirs and biographies are too many to list. From the constitutional point of view, Colin Shrosbree's book (1988) on the Clarendon Commission and its consequences for Shrewsbury is of the first importance.

It is doubtful whether, in the strictest sense, a full new history needs to be written, if by history is meant, for example, a renewed and detailed investigation of the vexatious litigation in which the school was almost perpetually involved for, quite literally, hundreds of years. But this book has rather different objectives: to tell the story of Shrewsbury School by looking at

Late nineteenth century photograph of the Old Schools, built between 1595 and 1630. The 1595 block was by the mason John Richmond of Acton Reynald.

some of the remarkable men who made it what it now is; by trying to highlight what is interesting, even exceptional, about it; by appraising as well as praising; above all by concentrating upon the key moments in its history – the abrupt discontinuities without which Shrewsbury School might or might not still be in existence, but assuredly not as one of the great schools of England; *en route*, some surprises may emerge. That is not quite all. The tradition of the 'Victorian' public school, exemplified above all in people's minds by Arnold's Rugby, was a durable creation, but it was not to prove a permanent one: the Shrewsbury that I went to in 1945 was very similar to, in many ways identical with, the Shrewsbury that my godfather had gone to a quarter of a century before. But by the 1970s much of the old order had been swept away, undoubtedly for ever. In this book due consideration will be given to this latest manifestation of the evolution – one might almost, with due pride, call it Darwinian – of the English public school.

It would be merely fatuous to pretend that, over a history extending now for well over 400 years, Shrewsbury has not had its share of failures as well as of successes, of problems to be surmounted, difficulties overcome.

Such episodes do not dim or belittle the far greater record of continuing achievement; rather, they cast it into sharper relief. That is not to imply that there are too many skeletons in the cupboard; to take a notorious example from another famous school, there is nothing to record such as the long-distant incident when it had to survive – and triumphantly did so – the dismissal of an early Headmaster, Nicholas Udall, for offences for which he might even have

The chapel and the school buildings. A 1952 photograph, one of several taken for a book which marked the school's fourth centenary.

had to suffer the supreme penalty. Adam Smith once observed that 'there is a lot of ruin in a nation', and so there is in a well-founded school. Happily Shrewsbury's problems have been less acute except, perhaps, at the end of the eighteenth century.

There are many ways, all valid, and not mutually exclusive, of telling the story of an academic institution. One way might be to emphasize the constitutional aspects; another to display and exemplify its physical and architectural features and growth. Yet another might be to concentrate upon the alumni, and a fourth to look at the men who helped to make the institution what it is. The 'mix' will differ according to the natures of the institution and its historian; it was only natural, for example, that J. B. Oldham should emphasize the quality of the Library. I believe that the facts of Shrewsbury as it now is almost compel the historian to lay the greatest stress on the fourth of the approaches touched upon above. To be sure, the constitutional aspects are very far from irrelevant; but the move to Kingsland seems to preclude any undue concentration upon the school's architectural features, and, for so ancient a school, the number of really famous alumni is not especially large. But as for the remarkable men who made the school, who saved it, developed it, transformed it: it is upon these men, giants in their time, that the historian must surely turn his keenest gaze, even though there is much else to be told – and that has not been told before. The rescue of 1798; the full story of the Clarendon Commission and its decisive implications for the school; the Move; the problems faced by Alington at his accession to the headmastership in 1908;

the post-1945 story, with the evolution of the 'modern' public school and the decline of classics: these will comprise the main thread of the narrative. What remains is, as so often, very much less than what could have been written: this is an episodic history.

Philomathes and Polymathes outside the Old Schools. The names underneath appear to be the wrong way round.

2

CREATION AND RE-CREATION

THOUGH one of the larger counties of England, Shropshire is almost the least densely populated, with little more than one head of population per hectare. The county town and administrative headquarters are at Shrewsbury, a town of under 60,000 inhabitants, if the latest edition of the *Michelin Guide* is to be trusted, and one which, despite the devoted efforts of a Shrewsbury schoolmaster not so long ago, still lacks a bishop of its own. Skirted by just one main road, the A5, Shrewsbury is still not especially easy to reach, and reductions in railway services have had an effect as well. What is more, Shrewsbury had no rail link at all until 1848, and no effective one until the lines reached Chester in 1851 and Birmingham in the mid-1850s. In terms of national importance, Shrewsbury's day has been past these several centuries, but its remarkable geography, being almost encircled by the Severn, and the location of a castle at the narrow gap where the river comes close to meeting itself again, made the town something of a natural fortress at times of war with the Welsh, or, for that matter, civil war. Did not Falstaff fight for a 'long hour by Shrewsbury clock' in 1403? It is not an obvious place to expect to find one of the nine public schools originally examined by the Clarendon Commission in the 1860s, only two of which, indeed, can be found to the north of London. Nor was Shrewsbury originally selected, back in the reign of Edward VI, as the home of one of the many new schools then being created following the dissolution of the monasteries and chantries. The story of Shrewsbury School has, as we shall see, almost as many twists as the Severn. It was not an easy nor a straightforward path that took the Schools (as the school is normally referred to) to its present location on Kingsland, looking down on where, to quote A. E. Housman,

> High the vanes of Shrewsbury gleam,
> Islanded in Severn stream.

How many Salopians have ever realised that Shrewsbury School has, in effect, been founded not once but on four separate occasions? These foundations – which might be termed creation, re-creation, transformation (1798), and transmigration (1882) – provide the four separate bases on which the Schools now stand. Without at least some understanding of how and why these developments occurred, no real grasp of the Schools' growth and achievements can be attained; but they must all be considered in their proper place. Whether other schools have undergone such remarkable changes of fortune, I do not know; certainly other schools have changed their locality (Charterhouse and St Paul's at once come to mind); but the chances which three times saved Shrewsbury are arguably unique.

REX EDWARDE . . .

Of the forty or so schools founded during the short and unhappy reign of Edward VI, a dozen can still be found numbered among those schools which are members of the Headmasters' Conference. Of those dozen, only one came in due course to be listed in Victorian times among the 'Clarendon Nine', or 'great schools' of England. That school was Shrewsbury (1552). It was no

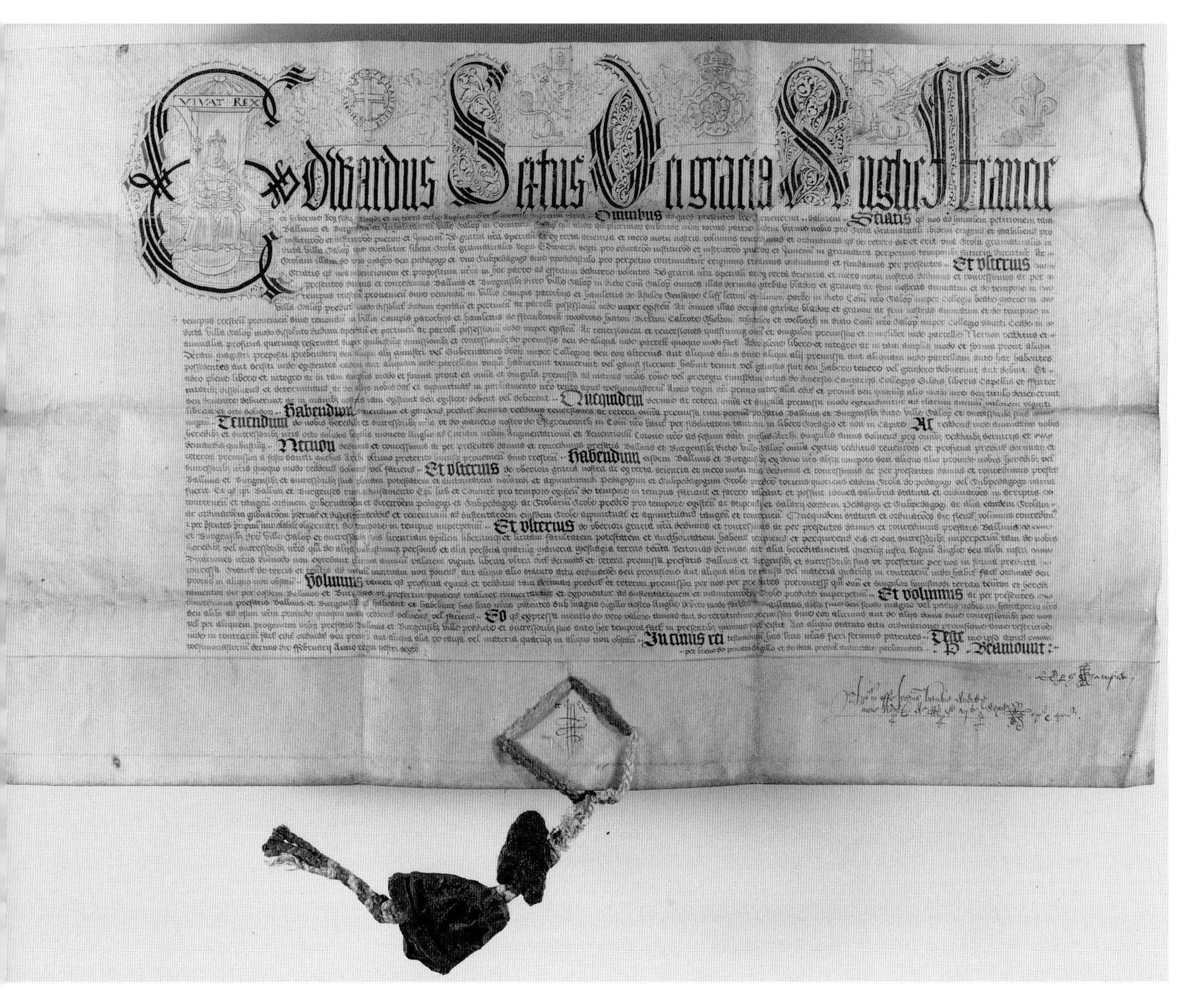

School Foundation Charter, February 10, 1552.

Edward VI, the Schools' founder, commemorated in stained glass in the chapel. The Old Schools' buildings can be seen in the top right of the window.

An early nineteenth century print of the Old Schools. Is the spaciousness illusory?

A recent photograph of the Old Schools, now Shrewsbury Library.

accident that so many schools came to be founded at about the same time, for many towns sought, in effect, to benefit from the Crown income resulting from the dissolution of the monasteries, while the further dissolution under Edward VI of many schools attached to chantries left another and equally severe gap, which it was up to the zeal of local towns or parishes to fill. So it was with Shrewsbury, where the Recorder supplicated in 1548 for the grant of a 'Free School' to the town: the term was later to cause much and prolonged trouble. The application was made to the Lord Chancellor of the time, Lord Rich, but despite the accompanying *douceur* of 20*d.* to 'a servant of the Lord Chancellor for his favour' in the matter, it did not meet with success. This had to await the passage of another two years when the united efforts of the burgesses of Shrewsbury and many other local or semi-local residents led to the presentation of a petition to the King in 1550 and then to the granting of a Royal Charter. The date is 10 February 1551/2; and the Charter included an important grant of tithes (which indeed would not become immediately effective) of 'the clear yearly value of £20 8*s.* 0*d*'. The Corporation accounts for 1551 show the purchase from one John Prowde, for £20, of 'a house and other lands and tenements' for the new school. The early Headmasters are but shadowy figures, and nothing is known of 'Sir Morys' or John Eyton, except indeed that their tenures were short, while that of the second-named was terminated at six months' notice. A school had been founded, but who (or how many) were its pupils, how they were taught, and by whom – these are matters of which nothing is known. Highly relevant, however, for the future was the clause in Edward VI's Charter which gave power to the bailiffs and burgesses of Shrewsbury to appoint the Master and Under-Master of the school whenever vacancies in those offices should occur (and also, with the advice of the Bishop of Lichfield, to make ordinances for the general government of the school). Yet it was rather as though an inoculation had been made, but, having failed to 'take', needed to be made again.

THOMAS ASHTON (HEADMASTER 1561–71)

It is only now that the history of Shrewsbury School can be said to begin, with the second foundation: 're-creation'. Ashton, a man well known for his abilities in the field of dramatic productions, was asked to produce, in 1560, one of the mystery plays that it was the custom to perform at Whitsun in the large area near St Chad's known as the Quarry. He was entertained by the bailiffs on more than one occasion and – we may assume – so impressed them that they invited him to assume the headmastership of the relatively new school. He was not a young man; he had been elected a Fellow of St John's College, Cambridge, as long ago as 1524, and must have been approaching the age of sixty in 1561. Ashton's main achievements – so influential as to lead one of the school's historians to say of him that he 'must be regarded as one of the greatest, if not the greatest, of the men that the School has had as Headmaster' – were three in number.

First, and spectacularly, he filled the school. By the end of 1562 there were already 266 boys there, and another 663 were entered before the end of 1570.

Nor were these purely local – half the list of 1562 were '*alieni*', i.e. from outside the town, and only 106 of the following 663 were '*oppidani*', or local. In those days of difficult travel it is noteworthy that early entries include names of boys from Buckinghamshire, Lancashire, and Rutland as well as – a little more naturally – Cheshire and Herefordshire. Moreover, we shall soon see that one of the school's most famous alumni was at Shrewsbury under Ashton; and Queen Elizabeth herself seems to have made an unsuccessful effort to visit Shrewsbury to 'see Mr Ashton's play, but it was ended'. The noted antiquary William Camden, in his *Britannia* of 1586, described Shrewsbury as 'the largest school in all England', adding that 'its flourishing state' had come about owing to the 'provision made by the excellent and worthy Thomas Ashton'.

But, if a school cannot survive without pupils, it has other needs as well: money and a constitution. Ashton's second contribution lay in his successfully obtaining from Queen Elizabeth tithes and other revenues amounting to an additional £120 a year: by 1578/9, total endowment income seems to have exceeded £180 a year. How this was achieved can only be conjectured; but it can hardly be irrelevant that Ashton's life was later to see him increasingly involved in politics and that he was already well known in high ministerial circles. At a time when life expectancy was so much lower than today, it is remarkable that, in his mid-seventies, he performed confidential errands for the government in Ireland in addition to other delicate tasks.

Ashton's third contribution to the school is to be found in the new ordinances of 1578. Ordinances drawn up more than 400 years ago, and superseded nearly 200 years ago, make for dry reading: what possible relevance can they have to a twentieth-century public school? But they must not be passed over, for they are indeed relevant to the school's later history. There is no need to set out here the ordinances in detail, but the salient fact is this: the new ordinances provided, in effect, for a tripartite government of the school by the burgesses of Shrewsbury, by the Governing Body of St John's College, Cambridge, and by the Headmaster himself. It will be recalled that the original Charter had put into the hands of local people almost all the control of the school, with the only real check or balance coming from the Bishop of Lichfield, a man doubtless with many other duties lying upon him. From the point of view of the school's longer-term interests, this could only be unsatisfactory. Hence the introduction of Ashton's old College at Cambridge, St John's; and in the new ordinances (subject indeed to certain provisos) the appointment of the masters was transferred to St John's. Preference, be it noted, was to be given to old members of the school, and local susceptibilities were bowed to in other respects as well. Yet if one can only feel it natural that academic responsibilities should be entrusted to an important academic body – though St John's had been founded no earlier than 1511 – it is perhaps surprising that the College also found itself with an important financial responsibility. While the town bailiffs and the Headmaster were entitled to draw upon the school's surplus revenue up to the value of £10 a year, any greater expenditure required the formal consent under seal of St John's College. Herein lay the seeds of future trouble, much of it political in nature.

For if in the early times, trouble between the town and St John's arose mainly because of tensions (arising from the differences between the first and second sets of ordinances) over the right, vested after Ashton in St John's, to appoint assistant masters, yet the later quarrels were to assume a political aspect, with the Whig Corporation matched, in the eighteenth century, against the Tories of College and school – a topic which could make for an interesting historical monograph. Finally, Ashton had seen how important it would be for him also to have the right to frame 'rules, orders and constitutions', and the indenture of Elizabeth had expressly reserved to Ashton this power for the application of certain important tithes and endowments; and he himself was undoubtedly responsible for the framing of the ordinances of 1578. In August of that year, within a fortnight of the sealing of the ordinances and his preaching a farewell sermon in St Mary's Church, he died.

Ashton's correspondence with the bailiffs reveals at times a certain sharp impatience, perhaps natural in one who was aware that, in the nature of things, he could not have long to live. Was it he who laid down that the curate of St Mary's should not be a common gamester or haunter of taverns or ale-houses or other suspect houses, nor should he be of any other known vice? Yet the ordinances are, finally, a monument to his good sense and to his study of the 'art of the possible'.

3

EARLY YEARS

WHEN Thomas Ashton compiled his first list of boys in the school, towards the end of December 1562, it contained the remarkable number of 266 – only half of whom were *oppidani*, or boys from the town – arranged in seven classes. Less than two years later, on 17 October 1564, are found the names of Sir Philip Sidney and his life-long friend and biographer, Fulke Greville, Lord Brooke. Sidney was placed ('tabled' was the term in use) in the house of one George Leigh, one of the town's two bailiffs, who had represented Shrewsbury in Parliament; not yet quite ten years old when he arrived, and son of the Lord President of Wales (who had his official residence in Ludlow) he undoubtedly received special treatment, and details are even preserved of the money spent on him.

The page of the 1564 school register where the names of Philip Sidney and Fulke Greville are entered.

No account of Shrewsbury School could wholly omit the famous letter sent to Philip by his 'loving father', Sir Henry. It may be thought a rather demanding document for one then aged about twelve to receive, read, and live up to (and the postscript from his mother is scarcely less daunting): but Philip was certainly a precocious boy, and it cannot be denied that he did his best to live up to the ideals propounded by his father:

> Son Philip, I have received two letters from you, the one written in Latin, the other in French, which I take in good part, and will you to exercise that practice of learning often, for it will stand you in most stead in that profession of life that you are born to live in. And now since this is my first letter that ever I did write to you, I will not that it be all empty of some advices, which my natural care of you provoketh me to wish you to follow, as documents to you in this your tender age. . . . Apply your study such hours as your discreet Master doth assign you earnestly, and the time I know he will so limit as shall be both sufficient for your learning, yea, and safe for your health; and mark the sense and matter of that you do read as well as the words, so shall you enrich your tongue with words, and your wit with matter, and judgement will grow, as years groweth in you. Be humble and obedient to your master, for unless you frame yourself to obey others, yea, and feel in yourself what obedience is, you shall never be able to teach others how to obey you. Be courteous of gesture, and affable unto all men, with diversity of reverence according to the dignity of the person; there is nothing that winneth so much with so little cost; use moderate diet, so as after your meal you may find your wit fresher and not more duller, and your body more lively and not more heavy; seldom drink wine, and yet sometimes do, lest being enforced to drink upon the sudden you should find yourself inflamed; use exercise of body, but such as is without peril of your bones or joints, it will increase your force and enlarge your breath; delight to be cleanly as well in all parts of your body as in your garments, it shall make you grateful in each company and otherwise loathesome; give yourself to be merry, for you degenerate from your father if you find not yourself most able in wit and body to do anything when you be most merry; but let your mirth be ever void of all scurrility and biting words to any man, for an wound given by a word is oftentimes harder to be cured than that which is given with the sword; be you rather a hearer and bearer away of other men's talk, than a beginner or procurer of speech, otherwise you shall be accounted to delight to hear yourself speak. Be modest in each assembly, and rather be rebuked of light fellows for maidenlike shamefastness, than of your sad friends for pert boldness; think upon every word that you will speak before you utter it, and remember how nature hath rampered up as it were the tongue with teeth, lips, yea and hair without the lips, and all betokening reins and bridles to the less use of that member; above all things tell no untruth, no not in trifles; the custom of it is nought; and let it not satisfy you that the hearers for a time take it for a truth, yet after it will be known as it is to your shame, for there cannot be a greater reproach to a Gentleman than to be accounted a liar.
>
> Your loving Father,
> Henry Sidney

Sir Philip Sidney's statue by A. G. Walker, erected in 1923 as a memorial to those 324 Salopians and masters who were killed in the First World War. The 224 names for the Second World War were added later.

A postscript by Lady Sidney followed:

> Your noble and careful Father hath taken pains with his own hand to give you in his letter so wise, so learned, and most requisite precepts for you to follow, with a diligent and humble thankful mind, as I will not withdraw your eyes from beholding and reverent honouring the same; no, not so long time as to read any letter from me, and therefore at this time I will write unto you no other letter than this, whereby I first bless you, with my desire to God to plant in you His grace, and secondarily warn you to have always before the eyes of your mind these excellent counsels of my Lord your dear Father, and that you fail not continually once in four or five days to read them over. And for a final leave taking for this time, see that you show yourself as a loving obedient Scholar to your good Master, to govern you yet many years, and that my Lord and I may hear that you profit so in your learning, as thereby you may increase our loving care of you, and deserve at his hands the continuance of his great joy, to have him often witness with his own hand the hope he hath in your well doing. Farewell, my little Philip, and once again the Lord bless you.
>
> Your loving mother,
> Marie Sidney

No one will doubt that the young Philip Sidney pursued his studies with all the diligence that was expected of him. What those studies included is happily known to us from Ashton's ordinances. Inevitably, the curriculum was classical, with such familiar Latin prose authors as Cicero, Caesar, Sallust, and Livy; such poets or dramatists as Vergil, Ovid, Horace, and Terence; and, in Greek, the Greek Testament, Xenophon, and that verbose orator Isocrates; no

Greek verse authors are listed, and Plato, Thucydides, and Demosthenes are notable absentees. It may be noted here that the Greek quotation which appears between the figures of Philomathes and Polymathes at the Old Schools, and in the copy at the Moser Building, itself comes from Isocrates' *Treatise to Demonicus*: 'If you love knowledge, you will be a master of knowledge.' (Less easy to identify is the source of the untranslatable school motto, *Intus si recte ne labora*, dating from the earliest days of the school; but the strained nature of the Latin combined with the ease with which it can be translated into a Greek iambic line has long led me to suspect a Greek proverb as the original.)

Sir Philip Sidney's fame has lasted to the present day; that of Ashton's ablest scholar has not. Andrew Downes, for nearly forty years Regius Professor of Greek at Cambridge, was (apparently rather reluctantly) one of the translators who produced the Authorised Version of the Bible. Variously described as 'a walking library' and 'the ablest Grecian of Christendom', he paid a moving tribute to Ashton, in the dedication of his edition of the Greek orator Lysias: 'After God and my parents he is the person to whom I am most indebted for all the literature I possess. . . . I consider it as a supreme, indeed an unparalleled felicity, that my father put me, when a boy, under the care of this most excellent person'; he had enjoyed the 'advantage of a preceptor of whom all his scholars may be justly proud': fine and moving words, which would be echoed some 250 years later in a funeral tribute to Dr Butler. Tributes to Downes himself from Joseph Scaliger and his correspondence (in Greek) with Casaubon by themselves provide sufficient evidence of his standing, for these were easily the leading scholars of their time. But his editions of Lysias and Demosthenes have undergone the inevitable fate of all such works. Downes died, aged seventy-nine, in 1628.

By that time, Shrewsbury's Headmaster was John Meighen, whose reign lasted for the astonishing period of fifty-two years. Its opening, in 1583, must have come soon after the regrettable suicide of a Welsh boarder, one Preece ap John, who hanged himself at the age of thirteen. 'An idle boy, and hated the school,' says the account given in the notebook of a later antiquarian Headmaster, Leonard Hotchkis. But who now can guess at what human tragedy lies behind that pitiful waste of a young life? By the time Meighen's headmastership ended in 1635, Charles I had been on the throne for ten years. It would have been surprising if so long an incumbency had not left its mark on the school; and Meighen's legacies were to prove enduring. The better part is to be found in the construction of the Old Schools (1590s and 1627–30), of which Nikolaus Pevsner approvingly observed: 'the new buildings are astonishingly stately. Few schools other than Eton and Winchester had such extensive and lavish premises.' For a school as successful and, indeed, '*numerosissima totius Angliae*' – having the most pupils of any in England – new buildings had become essential. Ashton, in the 1570s, had criticized the buildings which he had inherited as 'old and inclining to ruin'; and, having been bought by the school and subsequently adapted, they were clearly far from ideal. Under Meighen, houses were provided for the second and third

Old Schools: Top Schools doorway of circa *1630, after restoration in 1984.*

masters; the new buildings contained both a chapel and, importantly, a library; and a house was built some miles away at Grinshill, to which the school could migrate in times of sickness (the 'sweating sickness' so prevalent in those times; it caused suspension of school activities in 1575–6 and again for nearly a year in 1604–5). Such evidence as exists suggests that the house at Grinshill cost between £500 and £600 to erect, a very substantial sum; but it would be good to have more detailed accounts than appear to be available for the costs involved in the construction of the Old Schools. What is safe to say is that their erection, together with that of Grinshill, argues for regular and substantial accruals to the annual surplus. We have the list of admissions throughout Meighen's time, varying between 181 (1593) and 46 (1585), and – excluding the 27 of the plague year, 1604–5 – they average no fewer than 97.

But Meighen left another and darker legacy. Whether he was indeed 'a very contentious person and of a turbulent and mutinous spirit and disposition . . . faulty in many things, some of them not befitting the place of an honest man' (as was the opinion of the Lord Chancellor's Commissioners in a hastily drawn up Report of 1613) we shall perhaps be best advised not to judge. What is certain is that his lengthy disputes with the town authorities led to severe friction, litigation in the courts, and even some kind of a siege in 1608 of the school buildings. The quarrels arose over alleged infringements of Ashton's ordinances by the bailiffs (who certainly also seem to have made free use of the school's money both in initiating suits and in defending themselves), exacerbated by local Puritan tendencies, shown especially when Meighen had to defend one of his staff, Ralph Gittings, against charges of papistical tendencies. Another dispute, this time over the tithes at Albrighton, started in the reign of James I and, horrifyingly, was not resolved until Dr Butler's headmastership in 1825, some 200 years later. Meighen's resignation, long overdue, took place in 1635; retired on half-pay with a stipend of £20 a year (and what we might loosely call a 'golden handshake' of £100), he did not live long to enjoy his retirement, dying in 1636, probably at or near the age of eighty.

It would be agreeable to record that so successful and populous a school as Meighen had presided over had produced pupils who made a mark in the world, but such is not the case. To be sure, we find the names of some bishops, a few prominent lawyers, a Lord Mayor of London (Sir Thomas Adams), a distinguished mathematician, Arthur Hopton, described by the antiquary Anthony à Wood as 'the miracle of his age for learning', and one commander of a ship in the defeat of the Spanish Armada, Piers Griffith, who may even, later in life, have turned to piracy against Spain (whether his subsequent burial in Westminster Abbey in 1628 was owed to his earlier or his later exploits is uncertain).

Before the next Headmaster, Thomas Chaloner, was appointed, yet another unseemly and costly squabble arose, this time between the town bailiffs and St John's College over the latter's entitlement to make the appointment. The suit, decided in favour of St John's, cost the school over £170, and an interregnum ensued until 1637. Chaloner's erratic career started well, with the entry of 128 new boys in his first nine months and over 100 in each of the following three years. But with the outbreak of the Civil War in 1642, we find the Headmaster producing a fine example of bathos: 'Let my successor blame civil war . . . that academics mourn and are desolate, that colonies of the muses are desolate, and the number of Shrewsbury School for this two years is so small.' The presence of the King in Shrewsbury boded no good to the school's finances, and out of the chest there duly came a 'loan' of £600; the King signed a document acknowledging the loan and promising that 'we shall cause the same to be truly repaid unto you whensoever ye shall demand the same.' Vain hope! The debt is still owing; and a calculation as to what the Crown would now have to repay, taking interest at 5 per cent compound, produces a number of a size that one normally associates with astronomical distances in light years or, indeed, the National Debt. Chaloner was a Royalist of the deepest dye (he described a Puritan benefactor to the Library, in Greek, as 'the first of the Roundheads of the new cut'; complained that a volume of the High Anglican Bishop Andrewes's sermons had been 'basely torn by the sacrilegious fingers of a Scotch camp chaplain', and indulged in an Arabic imprecation against Archbishop Laud's Puritan antagonist, William Prynne). In 1646, the Parliamentary forces captured Shrewsbury, and the expulsion of Chaloner, together with the forfeiture of his goods, became inevitable. Nineteen years of nomadic (and not unsuccessful) schoolmastering followed; but his final restoration to Shrewsbury in 1663 lasted no longer than a year, and he died in October 1664.

Chaloner's time was marked by yet further costly disputes involving the school (notably, but not only, over the application of the Chirbury tithes and the stipend of the curate of St Mary's), with their inevitable financial consequences. It also included the sojourn at the school, from 1643, of George Savile, afterwards Marquis of Halifax, known to readers of Macaulay as 'The Trimmer', and fairly dubbed by Oldham the 'brilliant writer and sagacious statesman of Charles II's reign'. Chaloner himself seems to have fortified himself in local taverns against his troubles (confessed to in rather charming Latin in the School Register: '*convivabar; etsi sobrius tamen aegriuscule*', which suggests that, while just about remaining sober, he had done so with difficulty and had had something of a hangover next day). Across the lapse of three centuries and more we can divine something of Chaloner's character, at once choleric and convivial, impulsive and generous. For we must not forget his message to Richard Pigott, the Puritan who had supplanted him in the headmastership: 'My love to Mr Pigott, and my prayers for God's blessing to the free grammar school of Salop: Thomas Chaloner.'

4

DECLINE AND REBIRTH

1666–1798

The Growing Darkness

IT would take all the skills and sophistry of the most devoted Salopian to depict the next 134 years as anything other than a period of long decline, with only few intermissions. Here are such numbers of pupils as are known or claimed (for the school's Register from 1664 to 1798 is lost, probably as a result of the incompetence, or worse, of James Atcherley):

1665	'sometimes 600'
1719	26
1723	16
1735	85
1754	'more than 60'
1798	'1–2': '12–20'

The period sees, yet again, friction (notably between the town and St John's College) of a kind calculated both to lower the school's prestige and to damage its finances. Much of this had a political background (Whig Corporation versus Tory school, as already mentioned).

In so long an era there surface at least a few names of Salopians who made their mark, not always happily, upon a larger stage. Shrewsbury was the first school of several to be attended by George (Judge) Jeffreys, afterwards Lord Chancellor and Lord Jeffreys of Wem. He was admitted, with four of his brothers, in 1652 (thus just antedating the period of decline, for he came while Richard Pigott was Headmaster, after the expulsion of Chaloner). One of the school's historians, G. W. Fisher, has said that Jeffreys's severity in presiding over the five judges appointed to try the rebels after Monmouth's defeat at Sedgemoor in 1685 'has made his name notorious, and has undoubtedly caused his moral defects to be exaggerated and his unquestionable abilities to be ignored by many writers'. Perhaps so, but many anecdotes tell against this. For example, Anthony à Wood tells how, in 1684, one William Wright pleaded not guilty to the charge of libel, adding specifically that 'the king and duke are brothers in iniquity, and if Eteocles did ill must not Polyneices know of it?' Jeffreys asked him 'if it were Oxford wit' that also 'he should say that if

Magna Carta would not do it, Longa Sparta should do the business' (Longa Sparta being a long rope). Jeffreys typically went on to express doubt as to whether or not to bail Wright, arguing that his words were rather high treason than grand misdemeanour. Shrewsbury can have few grounds for satisfaction in having educated such a man, however briefly; however, since he was probably only 44 when he died in 1689 and may have been no more than seven years old when he was entered at the school (which he left in 1659), we may reasonably invite St Paul's and Westminster to share the odium still attaching to his name.

It is a relief to turn to such as Ambrose (Namby-pamby) Philips, whose entry into the school may be dated around 1685, and who was to achieve inclusion in Johnson's *Lives of the Poets*; to John Taylor, known as 'Demosthenes' Taylor (*c.* 1715), of whom the same Johnson said 'Demosthenes Taylor is the most silent man, the merest statue of a man that I have ever seen. I have dined in company with him, and all he said during the whole time was "Richard"' (thus disposing of a question as to which of two men with the same surname had made a certain statement). William Adams (*c.* 1715) became not only Master of Pembroke College, Oxford, but also – at least as enduringly – a lifelong friend of Dr Johnson. Charles Burney, the father of Fanny Burney, Madame d'Arblay, entered the school in 1737, was the friend of Johnson, Garrick, Burke, and Reynolds, and published a large-scale *History of Music*. So much we know; but the school was entering a dark era and we cannot tell what sort of lives they lived at Shrewsbury. Of Taylor at least we know that he left much of his large and valuable library to the school (a library not much later to be described as the best of any public school with the exception of Eton); and in Sandys's great *History of Classical Scholarship* a more attractive account than that of Johnson is given of Taylor, by his friend George Ashby: 'If you called on him in College [St John's, Cambridge] after dinner, you were sure to find him sitting at an old oval walnut-tree table entirely covered with books . . . he instantly appeared as cheerful, good-humoured, and *dégagé*, as if he had not been at all engaged or interrupted.' Perhaps Dr Johnson had given Taylor no chance to interrupt? For a man who was successively Librarian and Registrary of the University, a significant editor of two Greek orators, and first publisher and expounder of an important Greek inscription, was clearly a man of parts.

Yet decline was in train at the Schools. The headmasterships of Andrew Taylor (1664–87) and Richard Lloyd (1687–1723), both Old Salopians, despite lasting for nearly sixty years, have left virtually no mark, and the same is true of the briefer reigns of Hugh Owen (1723–27) and Robert Phillips (1727–35). Leonard Hotchkis was a man of a different stamp, though he, too, like so many of his predecessors, found himself involved in clashes with the town and expensive lawsuits brought by the Corporation against the school. But Hotchkis was no more able than his predecessors to ameliorate the dismal state of affairs, though at least it was not under his headmastership, but that of Richard Lloyd, that one B. Wingfield was removed from Shrewsbury and sent to Wem 'for his better education, as were several other scholars about that time, Shrewsbury School then being in low repute, and the Chief Schoolmaster at that time by his age and infirmities rendered incapable to discharge his duty'. Hotchkis was not only an antiquary but a scholar, the value of whose work on the difficult but important Greek metrician Hephaestion was recognized by the later editor, Dean Gaisford of Christ Church. The Schools, however, were not in need of a *scholar* as its Headmaster, and entries seem to have averaged no more than twenty-three a year, while frequent staff changes tell their own tale. 'It is a melancholy state to be in, and I wish to get out of it.' He resigned, after nineteen years as Headmaster, in 1754, dying in 1771. His legacy lies in his work for the Library, which he reorganized, making two new catalogues.

Virtually nothing is known of his successor, Charles Newling (1754–70), as usual an Old Salopian: 'a man of high reputation, peculiar charm, and of striking presence'. The school may have achieved a brief renaissance, with 'more than sixty boarders in his house' who 'highly venerated their worthy preceptor'. If so, it was short-lived; for under the latter years of James Atcherley (1771–98), the school was to come near to extinction, a fact which cannot be wished away, however unfair or exaggerated the anecdotes concerning him. Another Old Salopian, but from Magdalene rather than St John's College, Cambridge, Atcherley is said to have been intemperate in his habits and to have allowed the Library (to which, to be fair, he had earlier paid much attention) to be used for hairdressing purposes and to have given away its books to boys (the few that there were). Certain it is (writes Oldham) that the Library was so unsavoury that Butler, Atcherley's successor, had to have a book cleaned and fumigated with sulphur before he could lend it to a friend, seemingly because it had somehow been used for the purpose of the boys' hairdressing. Other books in the Library may have been mutilated and, disgracefully, it was in his time that the School Register containing the entries since 1664 was lost. It is hardly surprising that the considerable scholar and bibliophile, Dr Samuel Parr, describes Atcherley as vulgar and ignorant. Atcherley's headmastership ended when he had become physically incapacitated in 1798, and, by the time he died, probably in his early seventies, in 1804, the school's nadir had been passed.

From 'the best-filled school in England' to virtual destitution in 200 years, and that despite excellent buildings and a location which, before the coming of the railway, afforded at least a powerful basis for consolidation if not growth. 'It is not ships nor walls', said the old Athenian general, Nicias, 'but men that make a city.' So it is with a school; men of moderate stamp, their energies constantly absorbed by costly and time-consuming arguments of a quadripartite nature (involving the town, St John's, the school, and, on occasion, the Bishop of Lichfield), were unable to advance the school's interests and prestige; and, as ever, fell prey to the seemingly inevitable law that institutions which fail to go forward must instead go back. Yet within two decades of Butler's taking on the headmastership, Shrewsbury was again a great power in the land.

The headmaster's house, a drawing of 1774.

1798: *FROM A FLITCH OF BACON TO TRANSFORMATION*

The 220 years that had passed since the ordinances of Ashton had seen the school enjoy varying fortunes; but in 1798 those fortunes had reached an ebb so low that Shrewsbury School was to all intents and purposes extinct. It hardly matters whether or not it is true that the Headmaster from 1771 to 1798, James Atcherley, had as his favourite diversion kicking, with a colleague, at a flitch of bacon hung in the kitchen to see who could kick it the higher. It hardly matters whether the numbers in the school had fallen to exactly one (by tradition, called Doveton), to 'three or four', or, as seems more plausible, between twelve and twenty. 'There is a school [at Shrewsbury] . . . Within the memory of many, a headmaster has had there . . . not less than sixty boarders. This school was once the Eton or Westminster of Wales and of all Shropshire. Now the present master does nothing, and there are not above three or four boys belonging to this noble foundation.' In such disparaging terms did Dr T. James of Rugby write to the future Headmaster of Shrewsbury, Samuel Butler. For a long time new boys at Shrewsbury, preparing for their 'Colour Exam', had to learn by rote the names of the recent Headmasters, and in 1945 I (in common with a hundred others) would recite, without a pause, 'Butler

Kennedy Moss Alington Sawyer Hardy Wolfenden'. We could not know, and would not have cared, that our list started with the name of the man who, to all intents and purposes, had become the third founder of the school. This would not have been possible without new and drastic measures. Frequent and costly disputes between the town and St John's College and between the successive Headmasters and the town had stifled the school's development and crippled its once promising finances. There had been constant and expensive litigation over the tithes. Ashton's ordinances had, at last, to be replaced, having become 'inexpedient and ineffectual'. (The account of 1798 which follows is deeply indebted to the researches of the Schools' Archivist, James Lawson.)

To repeat, by the final years of the eighteenth century Shrewsbury School was moribund. The Headmaster was not only incompetent but ailing. The masters (such as they were) were occupying virtual sinecures. The constitution of the school was flawed, as it so long had been, with the Corporation, the Headmaster, and St John's College, Cambridge, all possessing jealously guarded rights and responsibilities which they were perfectly happy to dispute with one another, given an occasion, at the expense of the school. In a community, which, in town and country, was being effectively governed by an informed and reforming magistracy, the deficiencies of this once major school could not pass unnoticed, especially as members of the Corporation were Old Salopians, Old Johnians, and in many cases country magistrates used to committee work. As early as 1794 a lawyer, probably Thomas Loxdale the town clerk, whose family was well entrenched in local administration, drew up a report on the constitution of the school. While this was biased in favour of the Corporation, it highlighted the points at issue and rehearsed the various legal opinions which had been procured on knotty points. Although the status and origin of this report is not now known, its contents provided the agenda from which the Act of Parliament of 1798 would be framed.

In January 1798, Archdeacon Joseph Plymley sent a letter of the first importance to Dr John Mainwaring, not only rector of Church Stretton, but, more to the point, a Fellow of St John's College, Cambridge, as well as being (oddly enough, to our way of thinking) Regius Professor of Divinity. Plymley, locally an important figure (though not an Old Salopian) and a leading member of the Shropshire 'Enlightenment', wrote:

> I am glad to hear that a gentleman who has so strongly recommended himself to your approbation, intends to offer himself a candidate for a situation in Shrewsbury Schools. The low estate of that seminary has long been matter of great complaint in the town and neighbourhood; and a wish for its improvement has been very generally expressed. I was party to a conversation on the subject last week at Walcot with Lord Clive [the recorder of Shrewsbury], Mr [Joseph] Loxdale the present Mayor and the Bishop of Bristol [Ffolliott Herbert Walker Cornewall, Fellow of St John's 1777]; and I yesterday met a small party of Gentlemen at the Mayor's house, some of whom were clergymen who had been first at Shrewsbury Schools and afterwards of St John's College, Cambridge. This meeting was proposed previous to Mr [James] Atcherley's indisposition and with his knowledge and approbation, and was intended to consider if any, and what methods could be taken

to bring the subject before the several trustees. Mr Atcherley's present incapacity and precarious state of health naturally presses forward an enquiry of this kind; and I should be very glad to learn how it could be conducted with least inconvenience or trouble to the parties concerned. The Master and Fellows of St John's College are, I doubt not, equally desirous with the inhabitants of Shrewsbury, that the liberal endowment in question should produce the greatest possible benefit; but how far this can be done without some previous regulation is much doubted.

May I request the favour of you to introduce this subject to the Master and Fellows of St John's College, and to let me know their opinion? As matters now stand there are many possibilities that may defeat the success of the best qualified candidate; or impede his usefulness should he succeed in his election [perhaps because he might not be an Old Salopian, a Johnian, and a local man]. Though not otherwise interested in this question than as a well-wisher to the general good, I have availed myself of your friendship to state what it is conceived may be the best preliminary step, and procure a meeting at Shrewsbury, or at Cambridge, or in London (as probably least inconvenient to all parties) of gentlemen to enquire into the present facts and to consider of what regulations may be advisable or by what power the same may be carried into effect. I purpose being in London by the 12th of February at farthest, and shall then mention the business to the Bishop of Lichfield and Coventry [James Cornwallis] in so far as he may be concerned. I should be very glad to receive your answer before I leave Longnor, that I may communicate its contents to the Gentlemen in this part of the country who have so laudably given their attention to the state of the Shrewsbury Schools at present, with the hope of bringing forward such discussion as may lead to their future prosperity.

Mainwaring, who was himself old and far from well, forwarded this letter to the Senior Bursar of St John's College for laying 'before the Master and Seniors'. It may be that the 'gentleman who had so strongly recommended himself to Mainwaring's approbation was in fact Samuel Butler. For the idea of reforming the school by Act of Parliament had already been discussed in January 1797 when Dr Thomas James, Headmaster of Rugby and mentor of the young Samuel Butler, wrote to Butler in the letter already cited, explaining the situation in Shrewsbury which he had recently visited, saying that the school was worth £1,300 to £1,500 a year, and had an 'excellent house and school built in a superior style'. As the reformers 'have an idea of pensioning off the old masters' he thought Butler had a chance but regretted that it was 'in the gift of some college' – little knowing that it was Butler's own, St John's. The letter from James was a little premature, but during 1797 the Headmaster, James Atcherley, became physically incapacitated and discussions for the future the more urgent.

Plymley has already made his appearance; himself neither Salopian nor Johnian, he saw his role as a 'well-wisher to the general good'. But the driving force behind the reform of the school appears to have been Joseph Loxdale (brother of Thomas Loxdale), deputy recorder and Steward of the borough, deputy clerk of the peace for the county, and Mayor in 1798, in whose house, probably Kingsland House, the initial meetings were held. The members of the informal committee (including local gentry who were Old Salopians and Johnians) were probably those later named as Trustees (i.e. Governors) in the

Act. One of them, Thomas Eyton, had in fact introduced the young Samuel Butler to the Shropshire scene in 1795 when he employed Samuel as tutor to his sons during the summer vacation. At all events, an able and active group of men, used to working together, was formed. In early 1798 Loxdale and Plymley took the constitutional path to reform by consulting the Recorder of the borough, Lord Clive. They visited him at his house at Walcot, where they also met the Bishop of Bristol, Clive's cousin by marriage, who himself was a Johnian and a previous boarder at Shrewsbury. Then came Plymley's letter of 26 January 1798 to Mainwaring from which I have quoted at length.

Events thereafter moved very quickly, as agreement between all the parties concerned had been reached before 27 March when a petition to bring in a bill to reform the school was presented to the House of Lords. The legal business was managed by Thomas Loxdale (town clerk and elder brother of Joseph Loxdale) who was well versed in the procedures of private bills; in Shrewsbury alone in the previous fifteen years some six Acts had been procured. After some delays and considerable amendment the bill received the royal assent on 28 June 1798. It cost just over £800 to obtain and the balance of the costs, £500, was not paid until 1807. The first meeting of the new Governing Body took place on 5 July, when Archdeacon Plymley was in the Chair. By this time the outgoing schoolmasters had already resigned and their annuities were agreed. At the second meeting on 26 July the nomination of the Revd Samuel Butler (a Johnian but not a Salopian) as Headmaster by St John's College was announced, and he was in residence by 1 October when the first boys were admitted to the reopened school.

With this Act, the school moved into a more modern era. The restrictions previously placed by various preferential claims on the free choice, by the Governing Body of St John's College, Cambridge, of the Headmaster and Second Masters were removed. The important power of veto previously resting with the Mayor and bailiffs of Shrewsbury was transferred to the Bishop of Lichfield. Almost as interestingly, the sons of local burgesses were given the right of free education, seemingly for the first time – presumably a compromise clause. All assistant masters, except the Second Master, were to be appointed by the Headmaster, who, himself, effectively had to be in Holy Orders. Oldham's conclusion is judicious:

> By this Act a complete breach was made with the history of the past two and a half centuries, but there can be no doubt that some such drastic action was the only remedy possible. The government of the school was made less narrowly local, though the Trustees were confined to residents of the county, which was perhaps wise in days when communication was less easy than now. The choice of the two senior masters was kept in the hands of an academic body, and the possibility of friction with local interests was removed by transferring the right to veto from a municipal body to the Bishop, who might be expected to take a wider view. At the same time the Headmaster was made more master in his own house by being free to choose his assistants, and neither they nor he had to be chosen on the ground of their place of birth, education or residence. . . .

John Hiram Haycock's Gothic roof to the library in the Old Schools, 1815 (restored in 1984).

Seventeenth century panelling in Top Schools which retains the carved names of scholars from 1770 onwards.

SCHOOL GARDENS
This car park is strictly private

ANNO TRICESIMO OCTAVO

GEORGII III. REGIS.

Cap. 68.

An Act for the better Government and Regulation of the Free Grammar School of King *Edward* the Sixth, at *Shrewſbury*, in the County of *Salop*. [28th *June* 1798.]

Preamble. Letters Patent of *Edward* VI.

WHEREAS His Majeſty King Edward the Sixth, by Letters Patent under the Great Seal of England, bearing Date at Weſtminſter the Tenth Day of February, in the Sixth Year of his Reign, did will, grant, and ordain, that there ſhould be One Grammar School in the Town of Shrewſbury, which ſhould be called The Free Grammar School of King Edward the Sixth, and did thereby create, found, and ordain, in the ſame School to be One Maſter and One Under Maſter; and did, by the ſame Letters Patent, give and grant to the then Bailiffs and Burgeſſes, and their Succeſſors, of the ſame Town of Shrewſbury, certain Revenues and Hereditaments ariſing out of certain Diſtricts near to the ſaid Town, for the Support of the ſaid School, and did by the ſame authorize and empower the ſaid Bailiffs and Burgeſſes, and their Succeſſors, to make fit and wholeſome Laws, with the Advice of the Biſhop of Lichfield and Coventry, for the good Order, Government, and Direction of the ſaid School: And whereas Her Majeſty Queen Elizabeth, by Indenture bearing Date the Twenty-ſecond Day of May, in the Thirteenth Year of Her Reign, did give and grant unto the ſaid Bailiffs and Burgeſſes of the ſaid Town of Shrewſbury, the Reverſion of the Rectory of Chirbury, in the ſaid County, expectant upon the Determination of certain Eſtates long ſince expired; and alſo the Reverſion of certain Tythes of Corn and Hay, ariſing from certain other Diſtricts near to the ſaid Town, belonging to the ſaid Rectory, alſo expectant upon certain Eſtates long heretofore expired;

Indenture of Queen *Elizabeth*.

A

Opposite

Top: *C. W. Radclyffe's 1843 print of the school chapel from his* Memorials of Shrewsbury School. *The screen seen at the end is now in the chapel on the new site.*

Left: *Dr Butler's house at the Old Schools, Tudor style by Edward Haycock, pupil of Sir Jeffrey Wyatville. Butler's initials are carved in the gateway. Schoolboy humour had it that the SB was a Public House sign advertising 'stale bread, sour beer, salt butter and stinking beef, sold by Samuel Butler'!*

Right: *Trinity Chapel in St Mary's church, Shrewsbury. Also known as Scholar's Chapel, the boys allegedly sat here during services under Thomas Ashton's ordinances.*

The 1798 Act of Parliament which rescued the school from near extinction.

Atcherley retired to be Vicar of Lydbury North, a living under the patronage of Lord Clive, and died at Bridgnorth in 1804.

Under Butler, the Schools were about to enter upon a great era. The third foundation had taken place.

5

RENAISSANCE
BUTLER AND KENNEDY

BUTLER

OF THE many great English public school headmasters of the nineteenth century, who has achieved the greatest renown? There can be only one answer, Arnold of Rugby; and, in second place, perhaps Benjamin Hall Kennedy would be the choice of many, not necessarily for the most satisfactory of reasons. Yet Samuel Butler's achievement at Shrewsbury was arguably at least as remarkable as that of Arnold. When Bishop Monk wrote to Butler in December 1835, shortly before the latter's retirement, he said: 'There is nothing in scholastic history which can fairly be compared with your career except that of Busby [at Westminster], and he did not, like you, find a school with only a single scholar.' And Dr Longley, retiring Headmaster of Harrow, and afterwards Archbishop of Canterbury, writing at much the same time, referred to Butler's career as having been marked 'by a degree of splendour and success unrivalled in the history of public schools'. (We should perhaps bear it in mind that Arnold's headmastership of Rugby had begun only in 1828, though it might never have begun at all had Butler's earlier candidature for the post, in 1806, been successful.)

Samuel Butler, headmaster 1798–1863, who raised the school from its desperate state to one of England's leading public schools. From the portrait by Thomas Kirby.

Butler's portrait by Thomas Kirby, now in the Moser Library, painted when the subject was about forty-eight, is less forbidding than many Victorian paintings of schoolmasters. Butler was a man who enjoyed life; perhaps, in a sense, he enjoyed a gamble, for taking on the headmastership, at twenty-four, of a once famous school fallen on desperately hard times must have given him qualms – not that this can be drawn from the published correspondence, except, perhaps, in his asking Dr James, his former Headmaster at Rugby, for information and advice on school management.

Butler's education had taken him to St John's College, Cambridge, after Rugby, and his considerable classical successes at Cambridge had early marked him out for an academic career; when appointed by St John's to Shrewsbury, he had already become a Fellow of his College, though it must be remembered that in those days both fellowships and headmasterships were often attained at a much younger age than is now normally the case. At the same time, his friend Baron Merian's claim (in a letter of 1824) that Butler was 'acknowledged to be the best classical scholar of England' is simply absurd, even at a time when English classical scholarship was at a temporarily low ebb, and Butler's edition of Aeschylus, severely criticized by Blomfield at the time of publication, is tactfully passed over in no more than a trenchant footnote in E. Fraenkel's great edition of the *Agamemnon* (1949).

His task was quite different, and his skills lay elsewhere. Yet before we examine his achievement, it is necessary to record one appalling – one might even say unbelievable – handicap under which he had to labour for some thirty-seven years. St John's College had the right of choosing not only the Headmaster but the Second Master as well. The first choice, William Adams, from Pembroke College, Oxford, who was due to arrive with Butler at the same time and as much a newcomer as Butler himself, thought better of it, and did not take up the post. St John's second choice was John Jeudwine: it was to prove calamitous. To quote Oldham: 'From the start of Butler's headmastership there began the tragic course of impossible relations between the Headmaster and his chief assistant, which embittered both their lives for thirty-seven years, to the detriment of the school, the scandal of the town and the constant embarrassment of Butler's every action'. The men lived next door to one another, yet communicated only by letter, often in the third person, or occasionally through an intermediary. On one occasion, Oldham tells us, a meeting was proposed between Butler and Jeudwine, with two others to be present, one named by each of them. Other grave difficulties involved sending boys to, or then keeping them, in Jeudwine's House and class, not least because Jeudwine's income depended to an important extent upon boarding and tuition fees. Jeudwine quarrelled with other masters (an independent witness describes him as being 'of a somewhat ungenial, crusty temperament'), and formed an alliance, troublesome to the Headmaster, with his brother-in-law, who had formerly been Mayor of Shrewsbury. When one recollects the endless differences between school and town over the past two centuries and more, it is not difficult to see what an extra burden was placed on Butler – or what may have helped to prompt him to apply for the headmastership of Rugby in 1806.

Questions arise. By and large, the sources are 'controlled' by the Butler side (Butler's *Letters* are edited by his grandson, Samuel Butler): but were all the faults on one side? Why did Jeudwine never attempt to leave? Did St John's College – which could have dismissed Jeudwine – take no interest? Does the affecting tale of a deathbed reconciliation in 1835 owe anything to Butler's desire at that time for a bishopric? Can we not accept evidence – admitted by Butler's biographer – that Jeudwine was 'irreproachable in character'? Butler and Jeudwine were coevals, meeting at the age of twenty-four. The historians of the Schools understandably see more of Butler's side, not least because, with the greater authority, he conducted himself so properly and modestly. Doubtless Jeudwine was a very poor disciplinarian. But after the lapse of 150 years we shall perhaps spare a thought for a Second Master who must have felt himself blighted in his entire career by a bigger man whom he could never hope to succeed or supplant. The evidence is powerfully on the side of the Headmaster (and, in one moment of grave dispute, the Trustees, or Governing

Top Schools where evening preparation was held. The nearer and larger part of the room was Sixth Form; beyond the screen was Fifth Form. The headmaster's desk is to the left; at the front is the rostrum from which Sixth Form boys construed.

Body, certainly sided with him) whose patience seems to have been inexhaustible: what more might Butler have achieved without the constant distraction of internal dissension?

It is a relief to turn to the positive side of what Butler did for Shrewsbury. With Butler's arrival, be it noted, we have at once moved into an era that is in a sense recognizably related to our own. There is a sharp and marked rise in our knowledge of the subsequent careers of Old Salopians. External interest in the Schools greatly increased. The Schools' numbers almost at once started to rise from the arrival of Butler just before the nineteenth century had begun. It will be remembered that Butler inherited a school with, in all probability, 12 to 20 pupils. Recovery, though not dramatic, was steady; by 1814 there were about 70 in the Schools, by 1818 120, by 1821 160, and by 1827 no fewer than 285.

Butler's style of teaching encouraged a spirit of emulation among his pupils. This coincided with a similar spirit at the Universities; for example, the system of Honours Degrees divided into classes, after proper examination, came into operation at Oxford only in 1807: and it may fairly be recalled that the

Universities too needed a renaissance after an eighteenth century which, despite recent attempts, not wholly unsuccessful, at rehabilitation, was at best less than distinguished. Butler instituted regular examinations which governed the future form order of his pupils, including those in the Sixth Form. Remarkably, as Oldham observed, these seem to have constituted a major innovation, and we find Butler receiving letters from the Headmasters of Eton (Hawtrey) and Harrow (Longley, via the undermaster Drury) enquiring in the most interested terms about Butler's methods; indeed, as is well known, on one occasion, the Headmaster of Harrow even came to Shrewsbury, with Henry Drury, to listen to Butler teaching his form. This was in 1829; the letter from Hawtrey came in 1834, so it will be obvious that Butler's ideas and reforms did not percolate to rival schools with any great speed.

Great successes were achieved by Butler's pupils at the Universities, especially, and naturally enough, Cambridge. Detailed accounts appear both in Oldham and (especially) in Fisher's *Annals*; and the results were, by any standard, astonishing. Inevitably, the successes gave rise to accusations of 'cramming'. It is worth looking in a little more detail at the most famous of all Butler's successes: that of Thomas Brancker. In 1831, when Brancker, then still in the Sixth Form at Shrewsbury, won Oxford's coveted Ireland Scholarship, two of his beaten competitors were Robert Scott, an Old Salopian who would later be one of the editors of Liddell and Scott's great *Greek-English Lexicon*, and William Ewart Gladstone. There is extant a letter written by Gladstone on this occasion to his father, in which he says 'this has contributed amazingly to strengthen the prevalent impression that the Shrewsbury system is radically a false one', though he generously goes on to say 'however, we who are beaten are not fair judges'. At this point, Salopians had won the Ireland Scholarship in five successive years. In the course of a correspondence with Butler, the Revd G. Booth writes (April 1833):

> I had understood, from a man of known probity and simplicity of character, long versed in college tuition and in examination for degrees and scholarships, that the Ireland Scholarship had of late been almost exclusively obtained by your pupils, in consequence of a sort of routine questions into which the examiners had fallen, as being hackneyed in academic system and the habitual lecture-room questions; all or most of which were within the compass of boys well taught at the superior schools, especially your own, where they were so thoroughly initiated in verbal criticism and technical philology. That, to obviate this unfair monopoly, and give a due opportunity to the matured talent, knowledge, and taste of the more adult academic candidate, subjects for essays, etc., and other additional questions, ought, and would, be henceforth set; which would elicit the powers and acquirements of more advanced age and progress.

The Honours Board on which appears the name of Thomas Brancker who achieved the remarkable feat of winning Oxford's Ireland Scholarship while still a boy at the school. As a result the university had to change its rules for eligibility.

It is a pity that the examination papers set for the Ireland Scholarship before 1833 are not preserved in the Bodleian Library. I have inspected those set for that year and, with the possible exception of a fair number of questions dealing with relatively minute matters of grammar in two out of the eleven papers, it is certainly not obvious that schoolboys would be at any advantage compared

Not a Roman emperor, but Charles Darwin's bust at the Schools.

with undergraduates, and in certain cases (e.g. questions of style, ascription of authorship, and textual criticism) the opposite would have been as true in 1833 as it would be today. In 1833, in fact, the Ireland was awarded to the Salopian defeated in 1831 – Robert Scott – who, in addition to editing the *Greek-English Lexicon*, became in due course Master of Balliol.

But there was one Old Salopian, and that arguably the most famous of all, with whom Butler's methods did not agree at all: Charles Darwin, who entered the school in 1818, aged nine, staying until he was sixteen. As he was to write:

> Nothing could have been worse for the development of my mind than Dr Butler's school, as it was strictly classical, nothing else being taught, except a little ancient geography and history. The school as a means of education to me was simply a blank. During my whole life I have been singularly incapable of mastering any language. Especial attention was paid to verse-making, and this I could never do well. I had many friends, and got together a good collection of old verses, which by patching together, sometimes aided by other boys, I could work into any subject. Much attention was paid to learning by heart the lessons of the previous day; this I could effect with great facility, learning forty or fifty lines of Virgil or Homer, whilst I was in morning chapel; but this exercise was utterly useless, for every verse was forgotten in forty-eight hours. I was not idle, and with the exception of versification, generally worked conscientiously at my classics, not using cribs. The sole pleasure I ever received from such studies, was from some of the odes of Horace, which I admired greatly.
>
> When I left the school I was, for my age, neither high nor low in it; and I believe that I was considered by all my masters and by my father as a very ordinary boy, rather below the common standard in intellect. . . .
>
> Towards the close of my school life, my brother worked hard at chemistry, and made a fair laboratory with proper apparatus in the tool-house in the garden, and I was allowed to aid him as a servant in most of his experiments. He made all the gases and many compounds, and I read with care several books on chemistry, such as Henry and Parkes' 'Chemical Catechism'. The subject interested me greatly, and we often used to go on working till rather late at night. This was the best part of my education at school, for it showed me practically the meaning of experimental science. The fact that we worked at chemistry somehow got known at school, and as it was an unprecedented fact, I was nicknamed 'Gas'. I was also once publicly rebuked by the head-master, Dr Butler, for thus wasting my time on such useless subjects; and he called me very unjustly a 'poco curante', and as I did not understand what he meant, it seemed to me a fearful reproach.
>
> As I was doing no good at school, my father wisely took me away at a rather earlier age than usual. . . .

Darwin adds, however, that a book encountered at school, *Wonders of the World*, first gave him the wish to travel in remote countries, 'which was ultimately fulfilled by the voyage of the *Beagle*'.

Butler's curriculum was indeed narrowly classical; no philosophy was taught, and hardly any history, and the provision of a more general supply of knowledge would only, Butler believed, have led to superficiality and

Sunday Evening

My dear Whitley

I would have written to you before this. only I was aware this letter would be a sort of a "last dying speech & confession before my Lord Judge". & then those black words "infirm of purpose" &c &c sounded so very horribly that I could not summon resolution—but here goes: I am idle as idle as can be: one of the causes you have hit on, viz irresolution. the other is, being made fully aware that my noddle is not capacious enough to retain or comprehend Mathematics.. Beetle hunting & such things I grieve to say is my proper sphere

Darwin's letter of 1828 (to his friend Charles Thomas Whitely, old Salopian) when he was one of a reading party at Barmouth, cramming mathematics, prior to Cambridge entrance, in which he bemoans: 'My noddle is not capacious enough to retain or comprehend mathematics. Beetle hunting and such things I grieve to say is my proper sphere.'

mediocrity. But there was a practical side to him, for if the Master of Trinity College, Cambridge felt obliged to comment that 'Dr Butler comes here year after year, just as a first-rate London milliner makes a yearly visit to Paris to get the fashions', Butler was doing no more than what has now become common practice; and the results speak for themselves.

The lawsuit about the Albrighton tithes has been mentioned. Having started in the reign of James I, and having continued with 'intermittent periods of quiescence' ever since, it flared up again in 1806, costing the school £3,000 in legal expenses over the next seventeen years. In 1821, Butler made himself wholly responsible for the conduct of the case, and in 1825 a favourable judgement was at last given by the House of Lords: at long last something could be done about masters' salaries (the Headmaster in 1727 had received £80, in 1777 £90, and in 1807 still only £120; the Second Master received £80.

In addition a proportion of the boys' fees was paid to the Head and Second Masters). Oldham adds, with some feeling, that the 'maximum which could be earned by the most senior assistant master remained £315 till well into the present century'. It is interesting to note that tuition fees were eight guineas in Butler's day, rising to fifteen guineas under Kennedy; boarding fees were £42 and £52 10*s* respectively.

Butler instituted an annual Speech Day (for which not everybody will praise him) in 1821; a visit from the Duchess of Kent and her daughter, Princess Victoria, in 1832 is perhaps noteworthy for the hint of humour to be found in Butler's memorandum of instructions to the boys: 'In cheering, some little boys who make a hideous squeal are desired to be careful not to do so.' Butler's relations with the boys, his restoration of school discipline, the 'epidemic of turbulence' in 1818, and the 'Beef Row' of 1829 will be considered later.

In 1836, with health problems affecting both himself and his wife, he resigned the headmastership; he accepted the bishopric of Lichfield, but died in 1839. All business in Shrewsbury was suspended at the time of his funeral at St Mary's; the town bells were muffled; and 'the mass of the people were in contact as thick as the footways would admit'. So died Shrewsbury's great headmaster. It is sad that his statue, dating from 1844, so long a feature of the Moser Library, was destroyed in 1967, provoking the addition of a verse (by D. S. Colman) to the school song, *Carmen Salopiense*:

Ceteri dum magistrorum	Lesser schools to men of learning
Diligunt doctrinam	offer veneration;
Nos in morem Vandalorum	We to Vandalism turning
Edimus ruinam:	seek their desecration.
Statuamque pessum damus	Armed with picks we pound our sage's
Malleis armati	statue till we've wrecked it:
Ne tradatur quem pulsamus	Right ordains that future ages
Vir posteritati.	never shall inspect it.
Marceat Salopia	Let Salopia perish

(The translation is owed to Mark Mortimer; attention should be drawn to the first word of the ante-penultimate line. Who was Headmaster in 1967?)

KENNEDY

Benjamin Hall Kennedy, an Old Salopian who had won both Cambridge's Porson Prize and its Browne Medal (which latter as a schoolboy he was not allowed to be awarded) under Butler, was thirty-one at the time of his appointment; like Butler, he had been at St John's College, Cambridge (indeed, he was the eighth out of fifteen Headmasters to have gone there). As Headmaster he built on, and arguably even surpassed the successes of Butler, though he also had his share of problems, especially in keeping the numbers up – there were many new competing foundations, and we have seen that the railway did not effectively reach Shrewsbury until the 1850s. The seal was set on his achievement and that of Butler when Shrewsbury was included (soon after Kennedy's retirement) among the seven schools listed in the Public

Schools Act of 1868.

Kennedy has often been written about (he was one of F. D. How's *Six Great Schoolmasters*, and one of Alicia Percival's *Very Superior Men*; he was Dr Skinner of Roughborough in Samuel Butler's *The Way of All Flesh*, and the subject of lengthy reminiscences by W. E. Heitland in his *After Many Years*). He was a more considerable classical scholar than Butler, and his substantial *Latin Grammar* remains useful to this day (his famous *The Shorter Latin Primer* may well not have come directly from his hand). The stories accruing round his strong and sometimes bellicose personality are legion. Kennedy belongs to Shrewsbury, and it is ironic to reflect that he, like Butler, once applied unsuccessfully for the headmastership of Rugby (just why he applied is uncertain). He was described by the Public Schools Commissioners as the 'greatest classical teacher of the century'.

Benjamin Hall Kennedy, headmaster 1836–1866, from the portrait by E. T. Haynes after W. W. Oules. A remarkable headmaster and, especially, teacher of the Classics, whose Shorter Latin Primer *has been a source of anguish to schoolboys for over a century. He was described by the Public Schools Commissioners as 'the greatest classical teacher of the century'.*

This 'greatest teacher' did not bother to observe normal practice. One fears that he would fail the PGCE course (a necessary qualification for teachers nowadays). His sins of omission and commission were equally remarkable. Well known though his seeming deficiencies are, they will bear repetition. For example, he was

> habitually a quarter of an hour late for school, he had little idea of setting a nervous boy at his ease and helping him out, but frightened him by storming at him if he hesitated or made mistakes, so unfairly in some cases that once it led to a protest by another boy who thought his companion was being unjustly treated. He recognized and certainly did not discourage the habitual practice of the Head of the School construing through the lesson to the rest of the form before coming into school, which many might reasonably think would not encourage the individual's mastery of difficulties. While usually meticulous in his demand for grammatical accuracy, at times he would let a boy 'get away with' slipshod scholarship. Moreover, he never gave fair copies, he never went through a composition with a boy, he sometimes kept an exercise for weeks before he troubled to give it back, and when he did, there were rarely any written corrections or comments upon it. But he somehow made his Sixth feel the enthusiasm for the classics that animated himself, and inspired them with the conviction that to write Latin or Greek as the original authors did was an achievement supremely worth while.

So Oldham, that most judicious of historians.

We also have the valuable testimony of his pupil W. E. Heitland, later a distinguished Roman historian:

> [Kennedy's] triumphs as a teacher were beyond all question. That the Sixth Form took a fresh vigour in his hands was attested by the successes of his pupils during his earlier years, and loyally recorded by Munro in the first edition of his *Lucretius*, and by Bishop Fraser in his sermon at the opening of the new school in 1882. In this capacity he was unrivalled, but it was a 'one-man business'. In the middle of his career he was for a time disabled by serious illness, and the school declined. In his later years there was a marked revival: he was no longer young, but his fire was still burning.

An 1843 print by C. W. Radclyffe showing the Old Schools with the castle in the background.

I have elsewhere described the usual course of a principal lesson and its sometimes stormy phenomena, as the Doctor grew excited and his mighty voice resounded in the ample space of 'Top Schools'. What I must particularly note here is the speed and freshness of the lessons, largely due to the fact that there was very little reference to questions of formal grammar. There was a sort of assumption, quite unjustified, that a boy had all that at his fingers' ends by the time he reached the Sixth Form. When you understood how much was taken for granted, you learnt how to deal tactfully with passages out of which awkward questions might arise. A new hand would be less adroit. In earlier days to elude Kennedy's criticism was probably less easy, but in my time his keenness was often blunted by the wear and tear of long service.

Heitland also notes the considerable benefits to the school of being sent good pupils from other schools: 'It implies the powerful attraction of the Doctor's own personality, by the stimulus of which unselfish teachers in other schools desired their best pupils to profit. Incidentally it confirms my opinion that the work of the lower forms at Shrewsbury was by no means an ideal preparation for Sixth Form life.'

Boys are fired by enthusiasm; and Kennedy's enthusiasm about a good composition was generous enough to inspire any ambitious scholar; he is described as striding up and down the room with an exercise in his hand exclaiming, 'Wonderful, wonderful!'. One cannot be surprised that his teaching, in spite of apparent defects, produced marvellous results.

Perhaps Kennedy's character as a teacher is most generously summed up in the words of Moss, his pupil and successor as Headmaster: 'His own undoubting faith in the worth of what he taught, the irresistible contagion of his enthusiasm, his kindling, inspiring, masterful personality – these were the secrets of his strength. . . . He infused into the more susceptible of his pupils such a craving for thoroughness, such an abhorrence of inaccuracy, that to have been guilty of a false quantity or a false concord stung them with something of the poignant shame which attends the breach of the moral law.' The hyperbolic element naturally to be found in a commemorative sermon must be taken into account, but when all is said and done Kennedy's achievements, in terms of University successes, must be allowed to speak for themselves: at Cambridge, 23 Porson Prizes, 19 Browne Medals, 9 Chancellor's Medals, 19 University Scholarships, 11 Senior Classics, 13 Second or Third Classics, and at Oxford (where far fewer boys went) 3 Ireland, 2 Craven Scholarships, and several other University awards.

Yet it must be pointed out that Kennedy did not have matters by any means all his own way. Having inherited a school with nearly 230 pupils, he was to see this number reduced to only eighty-eight by 1851, whether because of his own illness, competition from newer foundations, unsatisfactory accommodation, or transport difficulties.

A Headmaster's life, even then, could not be solely devoted to teaching. As we shall see, the Public Schools (Clarendon) Commissioners visited Shrewsbury in 1862; while Kennedy himself gave evidence (at considerable length), so did representatives of the Trustees and of the town Corporation, and an Old Salopian, C. E. Graves, who provides valuable evidence on the amount of classical reading that a Salopian might reasonably be expected to undertake.

The Commissioners' most important criticisms were that the Corporation, which (to say the least) had a historic connection with the government of the school, was represented among the Trustees only by its annually changing Mayor, while St John's College, which appointed the Headmaster, was not represented at all; that free education for sons of burgesses, their preferential claims on exhibitions, and the limitation of the latter to certain colleges were out of date and a drag upon the normal development of a public school (a conclusion which they applied to all the schools); the day-boys should be regarded as at all times under discipline; and – by its implications the most important of all – that the school buildings and boarding houses were far below the requisite level, or, in the terms that Kennedy himself used, 'old, unattractive, and in some respects inconvenient and inadequate'.

Some of the Commissioners' comments are noteworthy. For example, they deprecated, in its existing form, Kennedy's experiment of a 'non-collegiate

Boys' names carved on panelling at the Old Schools. Notice the name Moser. There were six Mosers at the school in the nineteenth century.

Rifle Lance Corporal C. D. Maclean (Shrewsbury OTC, 1859–61).

class', because its tendency seemed to be rather to stimulate than to satisfy the demand for the virtual conversion of the Schools into a middle-class, non-classical institution. They regarded – a matter of much interest – the monitorial system at Shrewsbury as unique, in that (to quote their words) 'the distinct recognition on the part of the master of the representative character of the praepostors, and of their title to speak on behalf of, and to seek privileges for, the school is, as far as we can see, peculiar to Shrewsbury alone.'

We have now arrived at one of the truly crucial turning points in the history of Shrewsbury School. At the time of the appointment of the Clarendon Commission in 1861, the schools which it was to examine (with the possible exceptions of Eton and Winchester) were endowed grammar schools; the term 'public school', which had been in use only from the beginning of the nineteenth century, implied that such schools were accessible to the general public, typically because their *endowments* had been provided for the general public benefit, or, as was argued in the case of Shrewsbury, *local* public benefit. The schools were *grammar* schools, which meant, in short, schools to teach Latin and Greek grammar. Naturally, they varied in the wealth of their endowments, Eton, Harrow, and Rugby being particularly well off (but Shrewsbury, too, was not poor: the surplus in 1864 of £1,820 – worth perhaps £90,000 in today's terms – *did not include income from fees*). They also varied in their willingness to provide teaching in subjects other than the classics – those subjects which might well most benefit less 'gifted' boys and which, not without reluctance, Kennedy for a time provided to a modest extent at Shrewsbury. By the time the Clarendon Commission was appointed, the schools were becoming reluctant to admit the meaning of the word 'free' which appeared in many of their titles (including that of Shrewsbury), and poor local boys were, in fact, no longer attending in any great numbers schools which had become national institutions, and provided a secure road, via the winning of awards in the classics, to the Universities. This is not the place to go into invidious detail, but the fact cannot be avoided that public comment on the misappropriation by the authorities at Eton of its endowments was a prime cause of the setting up of the Clarendon Commission.

But the general concern was wider. What were the 'public' schools teaching, and whom? Given that they had begun to charge fees to most of their pupils (having gained a reputation, e.g. for scholarship, that attracted such pupils), given that a small number of them had achieved particular success (for one, or a combination, of a variety of reasons: at Shrewsbury exceptional success in classical scholarship, under two remarkable Headmasters), should their status be formally recognised? Should they be made, or at least encouraged, to improve their often dismal accommodation by the removal of the restraints imposed by the terms of their original endowments? Might not new Governing Bodies be called for, with greater willingness to promote broader curricula? (Though this final aim was to prove, for the time being, a pipe-dream; both Headmasters and (new) Governing Bodies, often largely composed of Old Boys, tended to adhere to the classical tradition.) Moreover, there had been disquiet about the known brutality that was rampant in boarding-schools, even leading, in one well-known instance, to death.

The initiative for the Commission came from Grant Duff, MP; the time was right, and his proposal met with surprisingly little opposition. Which of the 'endowed grammar schools' should be included? The Commission decided to examine just nine, as being those schools which, in their opinion, had a national rather than local reputation – Eton, Winchester, Harrow, Rugby, Charterhouse, Westminster, St Paul's, Merchant Taylors', and Shrewsbury.

And Shrewsbury: as a commentator has recently observed, 'the school was thought to be on the borderline between the schools of the Clarendon Commission and the other endowed grammar schools', and Grant Duff's comments illustrated the difficulties of defining the 'public schools' for the Commission on selected social and political grounds.

> This foundation now lies at the boundary line, I think, we may say, between the public schools usually so called and the other endowed schools of the country, and some controversy has arisen in recent years as to whether it should be adequate rather to the wants of the middle class, as of course the majority of the endowed schools ought to be. The Commissioners have decided that *it should remain a first-rate school* (author's italics), and I think they have decided wisely. . . . The Commissioners say that the people of Shrewsbury should turn their attention rather to creating a good proprietary school in the town, than to making the present school fulfil the purpose of an institution for giving what is loosely called middle class education.

Dr B. H. Kennedy and his staff in about 1860.

Some forty years earlier, Butler had put forward arguments along the same lines to Henry Brougham:

> It only now remains for me to shew that Shrewsbury school both was originally a Public School, and ought to be considered at the present time. And if I can prove this, then I hope I shall not be thought to ask too much, when I express a hope that you will use your best exertions to have it included in that list of exemptions from the operation of your [proposed] bill, on the ground of their being Public Schools, namely, Cathedral Schools and the Colleges or Schools of Eton, Westminster, Winchester, Harrow, the Charter House, and Rugby . . . 1. If by a Public School is meant a school open to the public, i.e. a 'school to which persons from all parts of the kingdom are in the habit of sending their children for education' (which I suppose is the most comprehensive and proper definition of the expression), this was the case in the Shrewsbury School at its foundation, and is so now. 2. Or one 'at which boys are educated in the higher departments of literature, with a view to their entrance into public life'. 3. Or, 'one of ample foundation, endowed with valuable exhibitions.' 4. Or, 'one in which the numbers and competition are so great, that the boys educated there distinguished themselves by obtaining public honours at the Universities; in this respect Shrewsbury School can produce lists which will, it is hoped, entitle it to rank, without disgrace, among the six eminent schools which the act specifically enumerates.' (No Act was then passed.)

Looking east in the chapel at the Old Schools, a photograph from the late nineteenth century.

The arguments which Butler had advanced could be put forward with even greater force by Kennedy. The school *was* included, and was later one of the seven schools (Merchant Taylors' and St Paul's fell out from the original nine on technical grounds) named in the Public Schools Act of 1868; and, thereby, its future was at once irrevocably transformed. It is tempting, but fruitless, to wonder what would have been the school's fate if it had *not* been included, but had remained among the many hundreds of endowed schools later examined by the Taunton Commission. My own suspicion is that Moss would have tried to secure the school's removal, would have failed and resigned, and Shrewsbury's position nowadays would not in essentials be very different from that of many other respected grammar schools. As it was, the Clarendon Commission and its enacted result conferred great status (and led to the creation, before long, of the Headmasters' Conference (HMC), which has grown and flourishes still). Shrewsbury's inclusion by Clarendon was a great coup, and one of the two or three most important events in the history of the Schools.

It could not conceivably have been engineered except by the record of Butler and Kennedy. But Shrewsbury was emphatically the marginal case, and the fact that the die fell where it did was also due to the fact that it specialised, with spectacular success, in providing the classical education at that time deemed to be the only one suitable for the 'higher' or 'ruling' classes, although, in truth, not very many prospective rulers in fact went to the school, nor did the local landed gentry habitually send their sons there, whereas the local professional and mercantile classes did. After all, had not the school been created by and for the bailiffs, burgesses, and inhabitants of Shrewsbury? So far, so good (though the Commission's specific recommendations concerning the school were numerous, detailed, and important). It was when the Commissioners' proposals came to be enshrined in law (the Public Schools Act of 1868) that the trouble began; for the Governors speedily recognized that Shrewsbury's inclusion under the provisions of the Bill meant that the school's local character would be lost, and with it such local privileges (notably, free education for sons of burgesses and preference in the award of exhibitions) as there were. The Governors themselves were all local men, and this too would be completely changed under the Act, while the school's very location would be allowed to be moved to a point within three miles of the city centre. Prospects for reform of the curriculum to make it more appropriate for non-classically minded boys became remote. The Governors, angry, tried to use influence in Parliament. They tried to make common cause with the Governors of Harrow and St Paul's. They made life very difficult for Moss, the incoming Headmaster (for, of course, this was the classic case of where the long-term interests of the Governors totally differed from those of the Headmaster), who saw the urgent need for a move to a better location. They simply did not want *their* school to become the nation's instead. But they lost, as was inevitable; the preferential rights of burgesses were to be steadily eroded and finally disappear, the curriculum was long to remain heavily biased towards the classics, the Governing Body was to become much more broadly based, with the Master of St John's College, Cambridge, as the only *ex-officio* member, and the school itself would eventually move to Kingsland whence its 'massive buildings' would overlook the town as a monument to the power of Parliament, and, one writer has recently claimed, to the divisiveness of Victorian class interests. But the same writer correctly observes that the school has 'national significance in the history of English secondary education as it was here that the break was made . . . between the old grammar schools of the country and the new public schools. . . . It was at Shrewsbury that an arbitrary line was drawn and the public school system created.'

Shrewsbury's somewhat delicate position is illustrated by the delightful correspondence on the subject of an inter-school cricket match between Shrewsbury and Westminster (quoted in the Fleming Report on Public Schools, 1944)

The Schools,
Shrewsbury.
February 27, 1866.

Dear Sir,

I write to ask if a match between Westminster and Shrewsbury can be arranged for this season? The most convenient date for us would be any day in the week beginning June 17. We shall be happy to play on any ground in London which you may select. Yours etc.,

J. Spencer Phillips,
Capt.

To the Captain of the Westminster Eleven.

Westminster.
March 5, 1866.

Sir,

The Captain of the Westminster Eleven is sorry to disappoint Shrewsbury, but Westminster plays no schools except Public Schools, and the general feeling in the school quite coincides with that of the Committee of the Public Schools Club, who issue this list of public schools – Charterhouse, Eton, Harrow, Rugby, Westminster and Winchester.

Yours truly,
E. Oliver, Capt.

To the Captain of the Shrewsbury Eleven.

The Schools,
Shrewsbury.
March 9, 1866.

Sir,

I cannot allow your answer to my first letter to pass unnoticed. I have only to say that a school, which we have Camden's authority for stating was the most important school in England at a time when Westminster was unknown, which Her Majesty has included in the list of public schools by the royal commission, and which, according to the report of the commissioners, is more distinctly public than any other school, cannot be deprived of its rights as a public school by the assertions of a Westminster boy, or by the dictum of the self-styled Public Schools Club. I regret to find from your letter that the Captain of the Westminster Eleven has yet to learn the first lesson of a true public school education, the behaviour due from one gentleman to another.

I am, Sir
Your obedient Servant,
J. Spencer Phillips.

To the Captain of the Westminster Eleven.

One result of the Commissioners' visit – and of the general impression received that, in spite of wholly inadequate accommodation, they were convinced of the high standard of education at Shrewsbury – was that numbers ceased to decline; they rose in a single year by seventy, and were, in fact, still on the upgrade when Kennedy announced his intention of resigning in 1866.

As is well known, Kennedy went on to become Regius Professor of Greek at Cambridge (and the chair of Latin there, founded at this time, has since 1911 been called the Kennedy Professorship); the first three occupants of the Chair of Latin were Kennedy's pupils, and the following one, though not an Old Salopian, was at least the author of *A Shropshire Lad.*

Kennedy died in 1889; it is ironic that the Greek verse inscription under his bust in the Library of St John's College, although by no less an Hellenist than Sir Richard Jebb, contains a metrical error which would surely have been outspokenly derided by Kennedy himself.

Charles Darwin's statue by H. Montford erected outside the Old Schools in 1897.

6

SCHOOL LIFE

1552–1882

ASHTON'S ordinances let us know the entrance fees in those early days: ten shillings for the son of a Lord, six shillings and eightpence for a knight's son, three shillings and fourpence for a gentleman's eldest son (otherwise two shillings and sixpence). Others paid lesser sums, down to the son of a town burgess – a meagre fourpence, less than 2*p* today. Divided by Ashton into three 'schools' – hence the 'Schools' of the postal address and ordinary parlance – the boys were allowed eighteen days' holiday at Christmas, twelve at Easter, and ten at Whitsuntide. However, a week's grace was allowed for the boys' return after the proper time of teaching had begun. The regular declamation by the top form of one act of a comedy displays Ashton's enthusiasm for the drama. Games there were, of a sort: chess, the long bow, athletics, wrestling. Sir Henry Sidney's well-documented visit of 1581, or an occasional pageant as in 1586, will have provided a welcome diversion from long school hours, mitigated by just one half-holiday a week.

Darkness now falls. Even the devoted labours of G. W. Fisher confess the existence of a blank for 200 years; and when light returned with Butler, it is not an attractive picture that is revealed. Startling instances of lawlessness disfigure the early years of the nineteenth century, and Butler's task was no easy one. And we must assume that Atcherley's dismal reign was anything but conducive to good discipline on the part of the few boys left in the school. Fairly or not, Butler speedily drew on himself the reputation of being a 'flogging' Headmaster; and, as John Chandos has observed, perhaps with a hint of relish: 'Whether the harshness of the headmaster drew reprisals from the boys, or the vice of the boys provoked the headmaster to resented severity, the result was a record of violence and crime without parallel in the great schools of the nineteenth century.'

In Butler's correspondence with parents complaints from the public are recorded over such issues as whether the coachman's whip wielded by a boy struck his victims with or without the wielder's intent. The complainants on this occasion were in no doubt that, as their spokesman deposed, it was the boys' 'pleasure to use a coachman's whip about them most lustily', and when human targets were out of reach of the whip, 'to pelt them most unmercifully with stones'. An anxious father was urgently concerned whether retribution was to be exacted, as he earnestly desired, by the headmaster, or, as popular

'Shell', once Sixth Form. The honours boards forming panels under the windows and facing the entrance are now in the entrance hall of the main school building.

outcry was demanding, 'by the common hangman'. In 1817 a somewhat sinister development is noted in recorded complaints against the boys. Salopians harassing villages from the top of a coach *en route* between Thornton and Chester, were no longer armed with stones, but with loaded pistols and proved quite beyond the control of the coachman. Local worthies charged Salopians with a catalogue of offences which included theft, violence to travellers on the public highway, intimidation, extortion, coining money, and consorting with criminals and prostitutes. By the beginning of 1817, Butler seems to have felt in danger of losing control over the 'savage denizens of his seminary' (Chandos again). On 28 January he wrote, 'I do not know how I can either confine the boys more securely at night or provide effectually for their good conduct in the day. I am at present lost in baffling and uneasy conjecture.'

In such an environment, theft between the boys themselves inevitably abounded, and a stage was reached when it was not possible for a boy to put down any article unattended for a moment without its vanishing.

Butler writes of beating in cases of '*furta Laconica* (daring but venial thefts) which you and I flog boys for with a serious face, and inwardly laugh at or admire for their intrepidity and spirit of adventure'. Chasing farmers' pigs and stealing ducks may fall under the heading of minor misdemeanours; the possession of bludgeons, knives, pistols, and gunpowder assuredly can not.

The year 1818 saw the 'epidemic of turbulence'. Other leading schools were affected; at Shrewsbury there was the strange case of Coltman. This boy, a praepostor, abruptly left the School with two others, apparently planning to sail for India. Their minds understandably changed, but Coltman – already dismissed for having sent the town crier round denouncing another boy's appointment to be a praepostor – wrote alarmingly threatening letters to Butler, returned to Shrewsbury and prowled in the Headmaster's garden, so that Butler requested armed protection from the Mayor. In a later letter, often quoted, Coltman wrote that his opinions 'far from being changed, that you are a paltry and despicable pedant, are and ever will be the sentiments of Thos. Coltman'. Coltman later reformed, becoming Deputy-Lieutenant, Justice of the Peace, and High Sheriff of Lincolnshire; but the episode leaves a disagreeable taste in the mouth. Again, in the 'Beef Row' of 1829, when all the praepostors were summarily dismissed for encouraging the entire Headmaster's house to walk out when the unpopular dish of pickled beef was produced, among those expelled were Robert Scott, Thomas Brancker, and W. H. Bateson (later Master of St John's, and first Chairman of the Governing Body under the Public Schools Act). In time, of course, all were restored, but more tact might have obviated the need for such absurdly drastic measures as Butler took.

And here we must take note that Butler was hostile to the introduction of organized sport; football was fit only 'for butcher boys', boating was rewarded with flogging, even cross-country running was strongly disapproved of. Two fives courts can have provided only minimal alleviation.

Kennedy understood well that extra provision for games was necessary, at once renting a playing-ground of about one acre below and behind the School. The introduction by him of single beds for all the boarders must have been welcome, if belated (of course, it meant fewer boarders and an accordingly reduced income), and the curriculum, which by now contained a modicum of ancient history and geography, was at once broadened by the appointment of a modern languages master. Mathematics became compulsory in all forms.

Printed programme for Steeplechases in the late 1840s, preserved in A. T. Paget's scrapbook. The watercolour has been painted onto the programme.

Whether or not the boys took part in the tercentenary celebrations (actually celebrated a year too early, in 1851), they can only have been glad not to have had to attend the dinner of portentous length – forty-six dishes are named – which then took place, not of course because of the lavish provision of food but because of the surely interminable oratory: there were no fewer than *forty-four* speeches. (Actually, school numbers in that year were very low, with only eighty-eight pupils – hardly an occasion for too much self-congratulation.)

In the time of Kennedy, games became for the first time properly organized. The Royal Shrewsbury School Hunt's Hound Books date from 1842, and the terminology, with the Huntsman, i.e. Captain of Running, Senior and Junior Whips, Gentlemen of the Runs, and Hounds, the 'pack', the 'coupling up' and 'throwing off', the fact that the first man home does not win but 'kills', is by then firmly established: we shall return later to the Hunt.

Shrewsbury's own form of football – douling, i.e. slavery, because it was compulsory – has rules dating from 1855. Those rules were distinctly idiosyncratic. For example, each side could consist of twelve – or of an unlimited number; a goal could be kicked at any height; some handling was permitted; and a tough offside rule led to much dribbling and encouraged 'the most egregious selfishness'. A later set of rules allows for an unspecified time limit; later rules still limit handling to the goalkeeper (of whom there could be more than one). Even the numbers on each side could be very unequal, nor was punctuality of arrival a *sine qua non*. With declining interest, douling continued on a House basis until the early years of the present century; it was already being displaced by Association Football by the 1870s, and the first inter-school match was played against Uppingham in 1876: the result was a goalless draw.

These are but dry bones. We are lucky to be able to clothe them with flesh. By a happy chance, the diaries of John Coker Egerton, a Salopian from 1844 to 1848 (in Kennedy's time), are extant, and give, quite literally, a day-by-day record of his life at the School. Egerton was no narrow specialist: running, rowing, cricket, swimming, 'rackets', douling (fifty a side!), fives, music, singing, Latin and Greek verse composition, and much else came equally as grist to his mill. The following few extracts give some flavour of the life of a 'good specimen of a Shrewsbury boy'; he was just fifteen years of age when his diary begins (with examinations in Thucydides, Homer, and Greek iambics) in 1844. On the day of his arrival he dined (i.e. had lunch) at the Raven (so, 101 years later, did I). Let us now let Egerton speak, all too briefly, for himself, while accepting that the full flavour of his character and life only emerge with a much fuller reading of the diaries:

Aug. 24 (1844) The match between the Schools and the Eyton Club, which was a mixture of the Wolverhampton Blues and Eyton, began. The Schools got 66. After dinner, when the Eyton was in, a thunderstorm came on which soon stopped the game. The lightning set fire to Mr Gough's stack, and, as soon as it was known, we all ran off there. Two engines came up and soon got a line of hose from the stack to the river and then played upon it. . . . About one third perhaps was saved. In the meantime the match went on: the Eyton got 79 with two wickets to go down. The rain again stopped them for good. I changed quickly as I was entirely wet through . . .

Sept. 4 . . . Went down to the Concert Hall and heard *The Creation* and *Stabat Mater* (Grisi, Lablache, Mario, Paltoni, Faventi . . .). When I came back I played in the match against the day boys. Got 16 runs.

Oct. 29 (1845) Fellows late from football. The Doctor said he would set 20 penals, but altered his mind. . . .

Oct. 30 Fellows late again. Doctor said he would dismiss the two head boys. Johnstone tried to stop blowing footballs in Gee's Hall. We all went in to the Doctor and had a parley. He annulled his decision. . . .

Nov. 6 Meeting of Debating Society. It was voted that Parliament were fully justified in calling William III to the throne.

Nov. 10 An 'extra' for the Remove as the Sixth had one. The Doctor laid up with his leg. . . . Hughes' circus came into town with a long train, elephants, horses etc. and vans. . . .

Nov. 5 (1847) Tomorrow being Holiday Saturday we went out with the hounds before dinner. I went as fox though, as we had no scent, it was a mere farce. Met at the Race Course and after a beautifully dry run by the river of about 2½ miles, killed at the same place. We began in the afternoon the fourth Georgic. In the evening the ceremony of roasting which is inflicted on all the new members of Head Room took place. Memo: nothing terrible. We afterwards had some squibs and crackers, the chief effect of which was a great smell and smoke.

Dec. 4 (1847) We did Greek, *Prometheus Vinctus*, before breakfast and second lesson instead of Mathematics. . . . After dinner I went down town and got my hair cut. I heard Hills try the organ before dinner. It is a beautiful instrument. In the afternoon a piece of pork pie was removed by one of the fellows from the kitchen and preserved with the intention of being consumed at supper. The Doctor, however, wanting this very piece for a friend who had come to lunch, on enquiry, discovered that it had been abstracted, whereupon at calling-over he sallied forth with a choice selection of epithets cut and dried which he vented with the utmost volubility upon the School in general and the unknown offender in particular. 'Filthy dogs' etc., etc. were a few of the characters we were for the nonce changed into. However the depredator restored the pie and with it, I hope, the Doctor's equanimity of temper which had been so unnecessarily ruffled.

Aug. 19 (1848) . . . First Eleven practice yesterday and today. I never get above five- or six-ball innings which makes it rather mild for me. . . . I went and examined the engine all over and had it explained to me by the man who

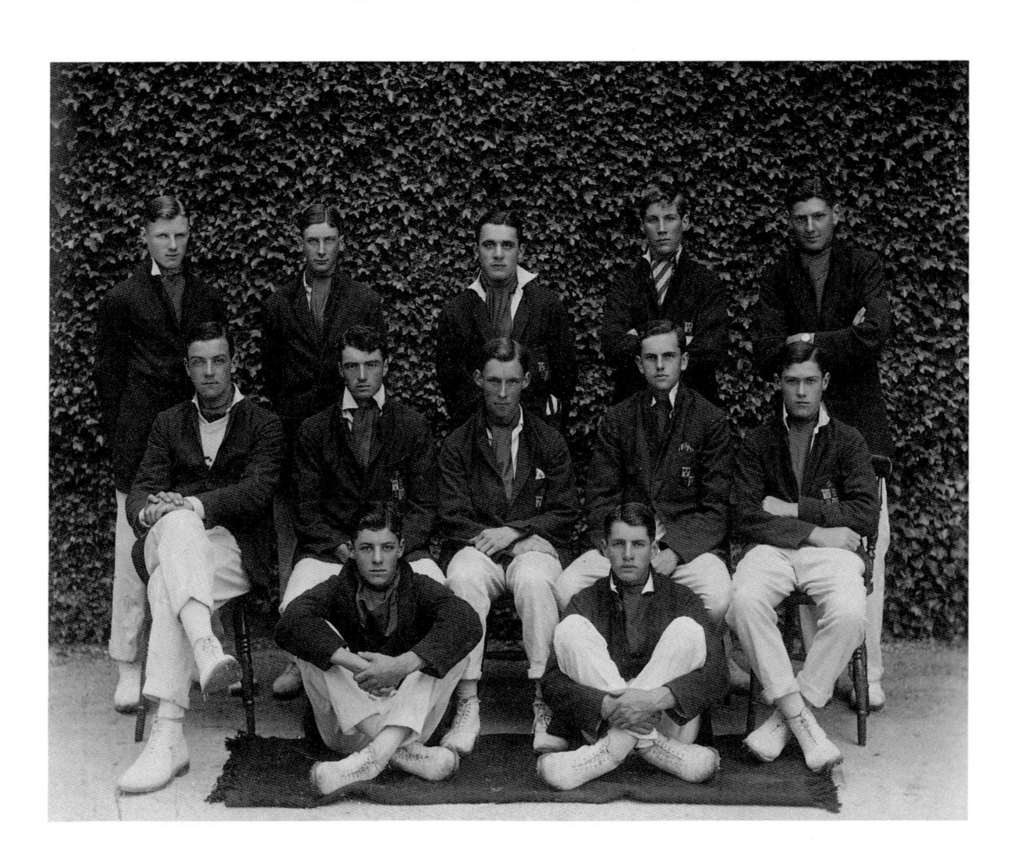

School cricket XI for 1921; the captain is J. M. Peterson, later headmaster.

takes care of it. . . .

Aug. 25 After third lesson in which we began *Plutus* of Aristophanes, I went to cricket, practised round-hand bowling and I can now get two balls following within ten yards of the wickets. Mrs Kennedy sent in a quantity of pears to the Head Room and both Halls.

In those pages, school life of 140 years ago comes alive, to show that the Victorian schoolboy did not differ in his enthusiasms, reactions, interests, desire for extra holidays, pleasure at success at work or outside the classroom, from those who were to follow him – or, doubtless, many of those who preceded him. Egerton, later in life, said 'I question whether any boy ever left school with a stronger affection for it than I did – I really loved the place.' That feeling constantly makes itself felt from the candid, unsophisticated pages of a diary which can be regarded as among the more precious possessions coming

Bumpers on the Severn.

down to today's Salopians from the Victorian age. Egerton enjoyed himself at a wide variety of sports and, defying chronology, it seems sensible at this point to add a coda on games in general – the playing of which had not been at all easy until the move to Kingsland, taking place as it did in an unsatisfactory field at Coton Hill.

A recent (1985) book on the public schools refers to Shrewsbury's 'great reputation for games'. The comment is not, perhaps, as flattering as it once would have seemed; and, upon reflection, the claim is not especially easy to justify in detail. The long tradition of the Hunt (RSSH) for cross-country running has not been matched by team or individual success that is out of the ordinary, though, to be sure, to be counted among the top six schools – not just public schools – in the country is no mean achievement. The obvious advantage of having the Severn on the doorstep has led, over the years, to a number of successes for School Eights at Henley, including, in pre-war years, two victories in the Ladies Plate, and three more or less equivalent wins since the war, together with two victories in the important Queen Mother Cup at the Nottingham National Schools Regatta. Even if this is perhaps little more than might be expected on purely statistical grounds, the school crews, expertly trained, have certainly performed with very high competence over a long period. There have been two Old Salopians who have won Gold Medals in rowing events at the Olympic Games, and just over 100 who have rowed (or coxed) for Oxford or Cambridge (not necessarily winning a Blue): indeed, no school produced more Blues over the decade up to the late 1980s, another proof of excellent training.

Well-nigh ideal conditions on the Common have, so far, produced no cricket international; the Cricketer Cup has been won on two occasions, and the Saracens were losing finalists in both 1988 and 1989. Association football internationals naturally date from the nineteenth century (an Old Salopian, J. C. Thring, is said to have devised the basic rules of soccer for the Football Association in 1862). More recently, there have been three outright wins and a drawn final in the Arthur Dunn Cup; and while a few outstanding players have shown themselves to be up to Football League standard, no mean performance, Blues have become markedly scarcer in recent years. Generous provision for Eton Fives has produced one really distinguished pair who won the Kinnaird Cup in three successive years in the 1950s. It is only recently that there has been worth-while provision for lawn tennis and squash. Golf is, inevitably, not a school game at Shrewsbury any more than elsewhere; there has been a solitary victory in the Halford Hewitt in 1980 (and a narrowly lost Final in 1989), but several more in the Mellin Salver for older players. The most distinguished athlete is obviously R. M. N. Tisdall (1921), who won the Gold Medal for the 400-metre hurdle at the 1928 Olympic Games in Los Angeles in what was then an unofficial world record time.

To sum up, however, Shrewsbury's record in inter-school matches – which are what count – is well above average, notably in soccer, fives, and cross-country running and almost certainly in rowing as well. But it would be quite wrong to see Shrewsbury as a sporting Goliath among public schools; quite

R. M. N. Tisdall, on the far left, at the Schools in the 1920s, winner of the 400 metres hurdles in the Olympic Games of 1932, in an unofficial world record time.

apart from anything else, the numerical preponderance of Eton – something like twice as large as Shrewsbury – would be likely to prevent that. To be sure, recent disappointments in the Arthur Dunn Cup, which Shrewsbury has not won for a quarter of a century, may be partly a result of geographical factors which lead to real difficulty in assembling the best possible team, which could then play regularly together in the Arthurian League. However that may be, the overall picture is one of healthily normal achievement rather than of the excessive emphasis on games which was more marked a feature of the public schools in the first than in the second half of this century. It is noteworthy that Moss, in the early 1900s, had commented that 'admiration for athletic distinction, even on the part of non-athletic boys, seems to me of late years . . . to have enfeebled interest in serious pursuits'. (It was a view shared by Dean Inge, who once referred to the 'vogue of athleticism, a puerile mania, deliberately fostered by schoolmasters' as being a serious impediment to religious observance at the Universities!)

The Hunt demands a little more attention.

Eton has its Wall Game, Westminster its Greaze (pancake ceremony), and Rugby's claim to sporting individuality is even stronger (and far more widely known). At Shrewsbury, the practices and terminology of cross-country running are unique and of at least 150 years' antiquity. Why, then, do 'couples' 'throw-off' from the Moss Gates? Why are there 'all-ups'? Who goes 'gently forward'? Why at the 'run-in' does a 'hound' 'kill' at the Column? Will the 'kill' be celebrated by a 'slay'? Who are the Huntsman, the Whips, the Gentlemen of the Runs? What do their insignia connote? Which 'horse' is eager to 'break first fence' in the Steeplechases, and who may his 'owner' be? What are the Paperchases? What of the Tucks and the Tucks Half? To many Salopians, just to say the words Bomere Pool, Cruckton, Longden, New, Lea Grange, Redhill, Bickton, Horton, or The Long is at once to recall autumn afternoons running across sometimes firm, often very muddy fields, wind against one outwards, if the prevailing weather does indeed prevail, and therefore mercifully behind one on the long way back. 'All hounds who wish may run in; run up and run well' – and so they have since the Royal Shrewsbury School Hunt, the RSSH, began (in all probability) in the early years of the nineteenth century; and most of the terms given above become clear as soon as the language of a hunt is translated into plain English. But in spite of the unvarying fox-hunting terminology, the Hunt has never concerned itself with actual foxes (or even hares) or hounds; foxes and hounds have always alike been boys, the foxes laying a paper trail as the scent. (The persistence of the tradition is the more remarkable given the opposition, in the early days, from farmers and school authorities alike.) As the names for the runs were mostly geographical, the majority of them were naturally changed when the school moved to Kingsland, and the runs were taken over new

The Officers of the Hunt, 1915.

Lining up for the start of the Tucks in 1921. Almost all the school takes part in this run, as do many of the masters. On the right is the unmistakable figure of the great rowing coach A. E. 'Bull' Kitchin.

country. The name, however, of the eponymous Farmer Tuck has been immortalised in the modern run, in which it is the tradition for nearly the whole school – and many masters – to take part.

The runs may seem long in mileage, as many of them indeed are. But a peculiarity of them is the existence in each of them of a fixed number of 'all-ups' – usually about four – when the whole pack waits for stragglers before starting off again. It is an obvious surmise that all-ups had their origin in the scent being badly laid, for it is clear from complaints in the papers of Henry Dryden that in his time (1832–6) foxes had taken to deliberately arranging artificial breaks. The result of all-ups is that the only actual race is in the run-in, after the last all-up, and this was so as far back as 1835. The run is started with the words 'Gently forward' from the Huntsman, and he regulates the pace, as, until the run-in, no hounds are allowed to go ahead of him.

Of course, traditions have evolved, endured, mutated, vanished. For example, Steeplechases survive, but not as once they were; for Henry Woodd Nevinson gives a grisly account of this peculiarly Salopian event under Moss:

> One peculiar custom may stand for many as an instance of the primitive barbarity which stamps upon any abnormal member of a herd. Since the last Pancratium was fought at Olympia, no such dire contest has been seen among men as our old steeplechase. Clad in little but gloves – a little which grew less with every hundred yards – the small band of youths tore their way through bare and towering hedges, wallowed amid bogs, plunged into streams and ponds, racing over a two miles of

The 1910 praepostors.

country that no horse would have looked at. The start was at the Flash side of the Severn, and if I had cleared the first stream and the hedge beyond it with one clean bound, as my young brother did, I would have it engraved on my tombstone: 'He jumped the Flash ditch. R.I.P.' The winner of the race was, of course, the boy who came in first; but the hero of the school was he from whom the most blood was trickling at the finish, and who showed the bravest gashes on his face as he walked down the choir of St Mary's at next morning's service. The course for the display of all this heroism was marked by the new boys, whose places as 'sticks' were allotted by the huntsman the day before, the whole school accompanying him, and by immemorial custom the most unpopular new boy of the year was always set at the last post – a slippery stump of ancient tree projecting in the very midst of a particularly filthy pond. As we drew nearer and nearer the place, all of us advancing at a gentle trot, one could see the poor creature growing more and more certain that he was the boy. We all exchanged smiles, and sometimes his name was called out; for all, except himself, had agreed who it would probably be. At last the pond was reached, and we stood round it in a thick and silent circle, awaiting the public execution of a soul. The boy's name was called. He came sullenly forward, and made a wild leap for the stump. Invariably he fell short, or slipped and plunged headlong into the stagnant water, whilst we all yelled with satisfaction. Wallowing through the black slush and duckweed, he clambered on to the tree at last, and stood there in the public gaze, declared the most hateful boy in the school. Upon himself the ceremony had not always the elevating effect at which we aimed. For I remember one disappointed moralist in the Fourth Form remarking, 'Frog's Pond doesn't seem to have done that fellow any good. He wants kicking again.'

Later, Steeplechases became less disagreeable and more ritualised: the account given below (for 1948) is typical. It is important to notice the formulaic way in which the results are declared; each 'owner' was deemed to have a 'horse'; all owners are called 'Mr', and so are the runners if they are the Huntsman, Whips, or Gentlemen of the Runs, i.e. have won their school colours for cross-country running. The initials of their houses would follow their names. The role of the 'owners', who would be garbed in every conceivable item of school or house colours that they could muster, was to accompany their 'horses' to the start, making such cheering comments as they could, and then to rejoin and accompany them on the 'run-in' over the last half-mile or so, encouraging their flagging mounts:

> Senior Steeplechases were held on Wednesday, March 3rd, at 3 p.m. The good conditions of the previous day had been somewhat marred by overnight rain and the damp foggy atmosphere. This year, the hedges were on the whole thinner, but considerably tougher and more formidable. As the School clock struck, there was the usual rush through the gate and along the bank to the first hedge. This was eventually broken by S. A. Barr (HR) with Mr Dowty (HR) a close second. At the top of the first hill Mr Bion (AET) was well in the lead, followed by Mr Treasure (WEM). Through the Ridgemount copse the order remained unchanged and became slightly more spread out, and through Tush's Hole, Mr Bion had a lead of about twenty yards on Mr Treasure, with J. R. Morris-Eyton (DJVB) third.
>
> Along the road and across the Craig Fields, Mr Treasure gained slightly, but after the second water jump, Mr Bion drew well away, and finally killed easily by eighty yards in a very fast time.

(The results then include the names of the 'owners' as well: *The Salopian* records that 'Mr Leach's Howe (WEM)' came in ninth.)

J. B. Oldham's *History* contains an admirably full account of the Hunt's long traditions and how they arose. In an age which has seen the ending of many such traditions, Shrewsbury retains the language and regalia of the Hunt.

CRIME AND PUNISHMENT

The control and direction of junior boys by senior ones was for many years one of the most characteristic attributes of a public school: Shrewsbury, where 'fagging' was called 'douling', was no exception. Indeed, when one reflects how few in number the masters are, even now, in relation to the boys, some form of control of boys by boys seems essential, and this was, arguably, even more true in the nineteenth century when six or fewer masters might have to restrain over 200 boys. 'Monitors' are referred to as early as Ashton's ordinances in the sixteenth century; under Butler they became known as 'praepostors'; these are school monitors, the term 'monitors' (after a period of differentiation on academic grounds between praepostors and 'school monitors') later becoming reserved for House monitors, who had lesser but still considerable powers (including, as recently as the 1950s, mild corporal punishment, used sparingly, and abused virtually never). There is evidence that, under Butler, praepostors were wielding real and independent influence in the School, as indeed they have continued to do. Butler himself, in a memorandum written in 1821, defined a praepostor's duties. He is one 'to whom the master delegates a certain share of authority, in whom he reposes confidence, and whose business it is to keep the boys in order, to prevent all kinds of mischief and impropriety, and to give up the names of offenders to Dr Butler, either when called upon by him, or without such requisition as often as they see cause.'

Kennedy went a little further, saying to the Public School Commissioners of the praepostors:

'They are a kind of senate or representatives of the School in relation to the Headmaster. . . . If a favour is asked for the School, or a remonstrance is wished to be respectfully made, they address themselves through the Head Boy to him.' (This representative character of the praepostors, in which they made on several occasions compacts with the Headmaster on behalf of the school, impressed the Commissioners as differentiating the system at Shrewsbury from what had been reported to them from other schools.)

Indeed, Kennedy is quoted as saying when he admitted a praepostor to office, 'If any boy should disobey a praepostor he would be considered to have broken a rule of the school', but he insisted that a praepostor's authority must be based upon personality alone, without the sanction of corporal punishment. Their privileges included being unrestricted as to bounds, going home a day early, wearing a top hat when other boys wore a mortar-board, and carrying a stick. The stick was introduced by Butler, probably in imitation of his own school, Rugby, where apparently it had been used for disciplinary purposes; it is still retained as an adornment. Hardy's shortened and amended version of earlier and elaborate praepostorial duties which inevitably became irrelevant and obsolete with the passing of the years is palmary:

> The duty of a praepostor (or school monitor) is to promote the welfare of the school, both by his example and by his authority. He is therefore responsible for maintaining a tone worthy of Shrewsbury, and for discouraging all such things as would in any way lower that tone. It is further his duty to see that the rules of the school are observed, and he is especially charged with the protection of the younger members of the school. He must remember that his duties do not end with his own house.

Only in the twentieth century has the Head of School come to be chosen on personal rather than strictly academic grounds.

There is no point in pretending that corporal punishment was not for a long time, at Shrewsbury as elsewhere, an integral part of school life. Butler, fairly or unfairly, early on gained the reputation of being a 'flogging headmaster', an imputation which he indignantly denied; yet to modern ways of thinking, Butler's claim in 1806 to have flogged never more than an average of twelve boys a year when there were fifty to sixty boys in the school hardly sounds like leniency carried to excess. Shortly before his retirement, Butler wrote to a parent to say that 'out of two hundred and sixty boys not three are punished (namely, by flogging) on average in the course of a week', which, if taken at face value, implies a sharp increase in the rate of activity, while other evidence suggests that even relatively minor offences led to a beating. Kennedy, for his part, was to tell the Public School Commissioners that he averaged perhaps a dozen floggings a year. (But Kennedy's preferred punishment seems to have been expulsion, followed by reprieve; at various times he 'expelled' all the praepostors, the whole Sixth, many Heads of School – and even, once, the whole school; but, sadly, the last story is no more than hearsay. On another occasion he invited to dinner on the same evening a boy whom he had 'expelled' in the morning.) All this tells us is (what we already knew) that flogging had a central role in the Victorian public school system. There is no reason to regard Shrewsbury as exceptional; one Headmaster of Rugby is on record as having flogged the whole of a form of thirty-eight boys within a quarter of an hour, and (rather earlier) the Headmaster of Winchester was apparently accustomed regularly to give up to fifty strokes on the bared backs of wrongdoers.

Douling, i.e. fagging, was abandoned, by mutual consent of the boys, by the middle 1960s; it had long been confined to one's first two years at school, and by 1950 or so the duties devolving on the last boy to answer the House monitor's 'doul call' were not especially arduous (e.g. taking a message to another House or, occasionally, cleaning a pair of Corps boots). Beating by House monitors was limited to three or four strokes with a slipper on a pyjama-ed behind, the victim having to be at least fourteen years old (failure to complete a 'Benjy's' run in the prescribed time or to perform the required number and type of 'changes' per week were typical offences leading to this punishment). Even Housemasters would, by 1950, only rarely beat a boy; and if the Head of House needed to administer a somewhat more severe beating with the 'biffer', a wooden instrument, he would inform the Housemaster of his intention (of course, he was thereby indirectly, but really, asking permission); such beatings were also rare, and three or four strokes were probably never exceeded. Of course, for really grave offences the Headmaster could inflict a beating with a cane, but in practice by the 1950s he did so never or only very rarely indeed. Corporal punishment has now long since vanished from Shrewsbury.

7

MOSS AND THE MOVE

Henry Whitehead Moss, headmaster 1866–1908, who masterminded the move to Kingsland, in effect the fourth foundation. From the portrait by Hugh Riviere.

To St John's College, Cambridge, there fell for the last time in 1866 the task of choosing Shrewsbury's Headmaster. Henry Whitehead Moss, a Salopian and a Johnian who was not yet twenty-five, had also had a distinguished career as an undergraduate. The third member of the great triumvirate – and the one with the longest reign, at forty-two years – Moss's real claim to fame lies in the supreme achievement, amounting to the fourth foundation, of the move to Kingsland. As a figure, Moss is not obviously appealing. But there is no doubt that his willingness to take the long view was of benefit to the Schools (a good example being his prediction that the number of pupils might readily grow to 500 from its then level of only 167 in 1884; 500 was reached in 1925).

Without a bursar, a secretary, a resident tutor, or a typewriter; taking almost the whole work of the Sixth; preaching every Sunday; the Housemaster of School House; taking his turn at school calling-over, detentions, and Top Schools (i.e. evening preparation), he did more than one man could possibly be asked to do. Oldham, writing in 1952, says that 'nine full-time men, helped out with the part time of a few others, have recently been required to do the work that Moss attempted to do alone'. We now must turn to the Move.

KINGSLAND – THE FOURTH FOUNDATION

The visitor to Shrewsbury who takes the once-attractive walk from the station to Kingsland quite soon reaches, on his right, what is now the County Library. Until 1882, this handsome building comprised the Old Schools; and if the visitor pauses for reflection (as well he may, for his walk will have taken him steeply uphill) he may feel at least mildly surprised that so modestly sized a building could often have coped with well over 200 pupils – indeed, in 1827 as many as 285, though many boys actually resided in other houses near by. It is indeed hard, even impossible, to imagine that, if Shrewsbury's future had had to remain limited to its cramped town site, it would have been anything other than unpromising. Decline would have been certain, and with the growing competition from such Victorian foundations as Marlborough or Radley, Cheltenham or Wellington, might well have been very severe.

The following account of the move to Kingsland is wholly owed to the admirable researches of the Schools' Librarian and Archivist, James Lawson. It need only be added that the Headmaster, H. W. Moss, was no more than twenty-five when he conceived the grand design (and in his mid-forties when

Dr Kennedy was a great enthusiast for charades. Three watercolours of the Christmas dramatics, from maths master, Revd A. T. Paget's mid-nineteenth century scrapbook.
Behind the Stage.

Upon the Stage.

Before the Stage.

it was carried through); and the reader may well find it helpful on occasion to refer to the map which appears opposite.

Opposite: *Map of Shrewsbury (1832) before the railway came to the town, showing the four sites considered by the school when they decided to move in the second half of the nineteenth century. Kingsland with the House of Industry lies to the south-west of the town; Coton Hill is due north of the town where the tollgate is marked; Belle Vue can be seen just east of south from the town; and White Hall due east, just south of the race course.*

The move of the Schools to Kingsland in 1882 is usually ascribed to the wisdom of Dr Moss following a battle against backward-looking Old Salopians and the opposition of the Corporation on obscurantist grounds. In fact although Moss had the sagacity and foresight to argue the absolute necessity for a move, the choice of Kingsland was forced upon him and the Governing Body by the Corporation backed by Lord Powis and the Chairman of Quarter Sessions. But for their implacable opposition and discreet diplomacy the Schools might have moved to the 'Arcadia of Coton Hill' and have had a very different history. The change of heart was due to strong practical and political considerations and to the collapse of the morale of the Governing Body following a major indiscretion by Moss in birching Geoffrey Loxdale and achieving national notoriety through questions in Parliament and versified merriment in *Punch*.

Although under Dr Butler and Dr Kennedy Shrewsbury had achieved an unrivalled reputation for classical scholarship as a public school, it simultaneously retained the constitution, buildings, and the disadvantages of a town grammar school. The terms of the foundation still demanded that the school accept the sons of burgesses as free pupils, although after the Municipal Reform Act of 1834 this class had become a closed caste whose privileges were envied and coveted by newcomers to the town. The strictly classical curriculum was for many inappropriate to their needs and there was agitation for reform which led Dr Kennedy to introduce the 'non-collegiate class' which omitted Greek from the curriculum.

The visit of the Public Schools Commission in 1862 underlined these problems as well as the primitive boarding conditions and general school facilities.

While the Public Schools Bill was under debate there was much petitioning and lobbying by both the Trustees and the Town. The borough objected that it was unjust to abolish the rights of burgesses to a free education as well as their preferential rights to the scholarships and ecclesiastical patronage of the school; rights which many of the middle and commercial classes of the town, who were not burgesses, felt should be extended to them. In effect the Public Schools Act of 1868 abolished these rights and created a new Governing Body which was far more remote from the town than the previous Trustees. This led to a feeling of alienation and frustration in the town which made the changes proposed by Moss after 1866 the more unwelcome.

The promotion of Moss, who had only spent two years in the school as a boy, was in itself a matter of comment. He was only twenty-five and unmarried; some of the senior boys had been at school with him as well as all the masters, who were considerably his senior in age. In accepting the post Moss made it clear to the Trustees that if the school was to survive as a public school, in competition with the new schools which were springing up, it would not be enough to redevelop the site as the Public Schools Commission had suggested, rather the school must move to the suburbs. In this he had the

Above: *Caricature of Moss by Philip Baynes (School House 1892–7), later on the staff of* Punch *and killed in action in 1915.*

Right: *Note the visual pun in this Moss caricature.*

full support of the Visitor of the school, John Lonsdale, Bishop of Lichfield, whose opinions were renowned for shrewdness and moderation. The buildings were in bad repair 'ill adapted to the present requirements of the school' and 'the surrounding circumstances are wholly unfavourable' . . . 'to inculcating habits of order amongst the boys'. As Edward Thring of Uppingham was to remark in 1873 'a boarding-school in a large city or watering-place is as admirable as a poultry yard in a fox covert'. Shrewsbury, as Moss well knew, had not been notable for 'moral tone' under Butler and Kennedy, and the lack of games facilities and the abundance of pubs and even less desirable attractions, made a move imperative. In 1873 Francis Morse said 'Nine out of ten parents who see the playing-fields of Rugby and Marlborough running up to the school buildings, and compare them with the school-lane at Shrewsbury, will not hesitate a moment in choosing.' As Moss remarked in 1868, 'the middle classes of this country have become more and more fully convinced of the sanitary value of spacious and commodious playgrounds', and boarders would only increase when Shrewsbury moved out of town.

Until 1868 the Trustees were unwilling to consider radical proposals, but then in January they agreed to consider removal 'whenever any practical suggestion be laid before them'; a clause allowing this had, on the suggestion of Moss, already been inserted in the Public School Act. Moss responded by proposing a site in Belle Vue owned by the Duke of Cleveland which the Corporation strongly favoured as being 'well adapted to the purpose'. Their motive then, as later, was the development of their Kingsland estate where villas for the middle classes were to be built, but before this could be done a new bridge was required and it was only in 1872 that this was promoted by leading townsmen and a private Act acquired in 1873. The House of Industry (now, of course, the main School Buildings) also attracted the interest of the Trustees in 1868 but to no effect, and little further was done until January 1872 when the new Governing Body, created under the Public Schools Act, first met under the chairmanship of Dr Bateson, Master of St John's College, Cambridge.

The new Governing Body lacked the inhibitions and hesitancy of the old and at once began to investigate new sites in Belle Vue, Coton Hill, Kingsland, and elsewhere, while leaving the option open to redevelop on the existing site. The merits of Belle Vue were vigorously extolled by the Corporation, whose proposals for Kingsland would be enhanced by having the Schools in Belle Vue as they would attract residents to the area. However, their case glossed over the fact that the adjacent suburb of Coleham was insanitary, unhealthy, disorderly, and a breeding-ground of typhoid, scarlet fever, smallpox, and other infectious diseases, as well as being the site of Burr's Lead Works, Trouncer's Brewery, and the thoroughfare to the new cemetery. As Moss observed 'not merely a poor but a low and vicious neighbourhood' which would not be improved if the military established a barracks at the House of Industry for 'it is not hard to conjecture what will be the character of the new suburb that will grow up between Kingsland and Coleham'.

As to Kingsland and the House of Industry, Moss had appreciated the beautiful position, but the proposals for a barracks ruled it out and he dismissed the site for 'the purposes to which the Workhouse has been applied are such that it is unadvisable that it should be made the nucleus of a great Public School . . . nearly all Old Shrewsbury men would shrink from the idea . . . and I am afraid that many parents would object to sending their sons to buildings on which such associations are indelibly stamped.'

Next in the field were the descendants of Dr Butler through their land-agent Timothy Burd who proposed a removal to the Whitehall site in Abbey Foregate, where prominent members of the Town Council had houses making it 'a most desirable locality for residence by persons of position'. Burd provided a neat lay-out plan for new school buildings, denigrated the proposed site in Belle Vue, and disposed of, or glossed over, all possible objections to Whitehall. By now the compass had been boxed. The Governing Body investigated the site and enquiries continued into February 1873 when they finally fixed on a removal to Coton Hill.

By September 1872 Moss was already convinced that Coton Hill was the only possible new site and he argued the case ably and followed it up in the summer of 1873 by soliciting the support of academic Old Salopians and public school headmasters. He understood the nostalgia which people felt for the old site, but the future of the school should not be sacrificed to the past and Coton Hill was preferred because it comprised the old cricket field, the original 'country' of the Hunt, the reaches of the river used for boating and bathing, and yet was still near enough to the town not to be impossible for the day-boys, although a massive opposition was to be aroused on this issue. 'Old associations' would be maintained and, as was observed to the Governors, 'it would undoubtedly be easier to come to terms with farmers for trespasses and depredations committed by the boys, where such trespasses and depredations are of long standing'. Once Moss had nailed his colours to the mast a well-orchestrated opposition arose from the Corporation, from nostalgic Old Salopians, and from discontented townsmen.

A committee of Old Boys, steered by leading professional men in Shrewsbury, opposed any move at all and produced an ingenious plan to redevelop the existing site to a design produced by Samuel Pountney Smith, a local Old Salopian architect. (It had a marvellous Gothic chapel adjacent to Castle Gates and an imposing Headmaster's house overlooking the cattle market and the Severn.) A massive petition was prepared and in December 1873, after much lobbying and noise in the local press, the Old Boys and the Corporation attended the Governors in London. The former alleged that it had never been the intention of the Public Schools Commission to remove the School, that the move would 'modify the teaching and usefulness of the School', that increased numbers might depress the academic standards, would militate against the day-boys, and was designed to extinguish them. This was compounded with a rather irrelevant reference to the loss of burgess rights, to the problems of flooding between the town and Coton Hill and to sewerage problems. As one venomous and inaccurate objector put it you could 'run races in coracles round two-thirds of the school enclosure during a very considerable portion of each year' and it is 'well adapted and is used for snipe-shooting'.

The petition of the burgesses presented by the Corporation was firmly rooted in the past, but the most cogent objection was made verbally by the Mayor who said that Coton Hill was an unsuitable residential area because of the proximity of the engine sheds of the GWR, the constant shunting of engines, and the nuisance from smoke. The removal 'would have an injurious effect upon the well-being of the town at large. It will prevent the Town Council carrying out their idea of letting or selling their land at Kingsland for villa residences, and that will be a most severe thing for the inhabitants.' The Mayor was ably supported by the Earl of Powis and by the Chairman of Quarter Sessions, J. R. Kenyon of Pradoe, who, as a burgess, was eloquent on the 'great injustice and wrong' that had already been inflicted on the burgesses. Despite heated opposition the Governors were adamant and during early 1874 commissioned reports on Coton Hill from a leading architect, Alfred Waterhouse, and Robert Rawlinson, the engineer to the Local Government Board. At the same time Powis and Kenyon took seats on the Governing Body and attempted to persuade the Governors to consider a better site, and followed this by suggesting that enquiries should be made as to availability of land on Kingsland, but to no avail. As a last shot at Coton Hill virtually all the medical men of any eminence in the town signed a letter condemning the site as unhealthy, damp, and a breeding ground for malaria. Like the rest of the correspondence it was published, but the Governors remained adamant.

The birching scandal which broke in July 1874 achieved national notoriety. Moss, sarcastically called the 'hero of the birch' by one of his most venomous opponents, had given Geoffrey Loxdale, son of John Loxdale the head of a leading Salopian family, eighty-eight strokes (for a drinking offence) to very little physical effect, but to the outrage of his parents, who called for an enquiry. (On the same day, Moss had administered forty-nine strokes to another unfortunate.) This was conducted publicly in the Shirehall where the Loxdales were represented by G. M. Salt, the secretary to Old Boy opposition to the move, who called Samuel Wood, the leading surgeon at the Salop Infirmary, to give evidence as to the severity of the beating; he was one of the principal signatories of the letter by the medical men in March. Although Moss emerged relatively unscathed from the ordeal, the enquiry was humiliating for the Governing Body and it made them think very hard about the implacable opposition of the townspeople to the move to Coton Hill, and when they met after a lapse of almost six months in December 1874 they discussed the move at length. They stood by their resolve to move but in view of the determined opposition to Coton Hill they took up the olive branch offered earlier by Powis and Kenyon 'that a third site, that at Kingsland might reconcile', and the Chairman was empowered to negotiate with the Mayor to this effect. A swift and cordial exchange of letters ensued which led to a deal with the Corporation and the Shrewsbury parishes owning the House of Industry so that by March 1875 the move to Kingsland was assured.

There were still many problems: the Kingsland Bridge Company had difficulties and had to obtain a second Act of Parliament, the old Shrewsbury Show which used Kingsland every year had to be ended, by the Home Secretary, having become a major public nuisance, and the Beehive pub had to be closed and the owners compensated. Prospective parents had to be reassured of the safety of the old workhouse for their children and the 'sanitary' problem was solved for Moss by Arthur Blomfield who prescribed new plaster, ceilings, doors, windows and floors to exorcise the paupers. The finances at the disposal of the Governors were limited and consequently the two boarding Houses, now Churchill's and Rigg's, were built at the cost of their Housemasters on a building lease. The cricket-ground was levelled by boys under the direction of A. H. Gilkes, later Headmaster of Dulwich, and the pavilion, shop, fives courts, and boat-house were paid for from subscriptions raised by Old Salopians with no help from the Governing Body. Money was so short that the Chapel was designed to be built in stages and although the chancel was paid for by the Kennedy Memorial Trustees the windows were plain and the furnishings stark, but to maintain continuity Moss brought the old screen, pulpit and communion rails from the old site. He recreated the old Top Schools but rejected the old school furniture as 'incongruous'. 'I wish to make a firm stand against the evil tradition of cutting and hacking the desks and forms, I had rather not be embarrassed by articles of furniture so full of suggestiveness.'

Except for the Chapel the new site was ready for occupation by April 1882 when the removal took place. The formal opening in late July coincided with

"SALOPIENSES FLAGELLATI."

(*Times, Friday.*)

ALAS that boys should be so tough,
Or Heads of Schools so kind!
'Tis hard to lay on stripes enough
To leave a smart behind.

The youngster, after eighty-eight
Light touches on his skin,
Rows out upon the Severn straight,
Perhaps a race to win!

O ghost of KEATE, appear and say,
How check the school-boy's tricks,
If four-score strokes won't do to-day
What you achieved with six!

Your fine Orbilian power rebukes
Head Masters such as these:
Into senarians you flogged Dukes,
And Bishops into sees.

And Shrewsbury would ne'er have seen
So charming a *Corolla*,
Had its Greek-loving Doctor been
Powerless to make boys holloa.

False quantity so hated he,
They who in *that* got fishing,
Soon found out one *true* quantity—
The quantity of swishing!

But there are those, though learned in
The needful Greek and Latin,
Who seem to touch a school-boy's skin
As if 'twere ladies' satin.

Head Masters now, 'tis very odd,
Are growing over mild:
They ought (see HOOD) to spoil the rod
Rather than spare the child.

And Shrewsbury its chief not less
Will prize, but yet more highly,
If he will practise in recess
Upon some *corpus vile.*

Some blockhead pachydermatous
His gentle arm must wallop
Secundum artem, till he thus
Restore the fame of Salop.

Nor think, though Poesy 's unborn,
That flogging comes by nature.
It is an art, which they that scorn
Ne'er in it reach full stature.

Birch-accent turns on divers sorts
Of nicely ordered circēs;
And much on well-packed longs and shorts
Depends, in rods, as verses.

Well-sorted twigs will sting, draw blood,
Yet thence no bruise endures;
And if you choose them thick in bud,
A good blow it ensures.

When Moss has learnt the Birching Art,
To LOXDALES yet in blade,
Six cuts, laid well, will cause more smart
Than eighty-eight ill laid.

Verses published in Punch *of 8 August 1874, inspired by the birching scandal.*

Churchill's, designed by the idiosyncratic William White of Wimpole Street.

the opening of the Kingsland Bridge, and with the completion of both projects the Corporation could look forward to the development of their Kingsland estates, which they did to the great profit of the town. In the end both Moss and the Corporation could congratulate themselves on their wisdom, though the path to Kingsland had been by no means smooth.

The completeness of this account renders further comment unnecessary. Many buildings have of course been added to the Site (as it will henceforth be referred to) over the past century, in response to the growing and changing needs of an organism which (to strain a metaphor) must never rest upon its laurels for too long. Further land, too, has been acquired, so that the Site has been extended to over 100 acres, in a homogeneous and relatively compact area. Yet (as Oldham tells us) an Old Salopian Vicar of St Chad's, the Revd J. S. Yardley, used to go so far as to interpolate in the Bidding Prayer, after the mention of the Schools, the words 'now unhappily removed to the heights of Kingsland'. Yardley did not have time to take a more charitable view, for he died, aged only thirty-one, in 1884.

It is said that Moss's relations with the boys were 'correct' rather than cordial. His personality does not come down to us as attractively as do those of some of his predecessors, though the general impression of coolness is mitigated by a few instances of not very remarkable wit; and the memoir written by his widow is, unsurprisingly, of a hero-worshipping rather than illuminating nature.

It is tempting to contrast Moss with his two predecessors by an irreverent look at their behaviour in church. Whereas Butler was pulled up by Blomfield, Bishop of Chester, for sharpening his pencil during service, in readiness for the serious work of correcting exercises; whereas Kennedy, while walking up the aisle in procession as Canon of Ely was heard to observe (the organ inconveniently stopping) to the canon at his side: 'Yes, I have found it a very nice after-dinner wine'; from Moss we have in full (in the memoir) a desperately mawkish sermon delivered on the death of a boy at the Schools – the sort of sermon which, as Oscar Wilde observed of the account of the death of Little Nell, one challenges anyone to read without bursting into laughter. Nor could one imagine Moss saying, as Butler did on going into his form room, and seeing the words 'Butler is an old fool' written on the blackboard: 'The melancholy truth stares me in the face.'

Perhaps it does not matter very much: the Salopian who enters the Site via the Moss Gates will know that by the energy, determination, and dedication of one man Shrewsbury School was not allowed to relapse into the status (however respectable) of a country grammar school. Moss, no lover of games, yet gave the Schools its swimming-pool; he introduced the three-term year (to us seeming so inevitable); the 27 acres have grown into a hundred and more; the numbers have grown nearly fourfold; a new boarding House was on the point of completion as these words were written, and Shrewsbury is among the most fortunately located of all England's public schools: all this is owed to Moss. Other schools can, with justice, point to truly great Headmasters, whether it be Eton's Keate, Westminster's Busby, Rugby's Arnold, or

The school choir in July 1897.

'Call not the fire a great disaster;
It was a blessing in disguise.
It has suggested to my master
The subject for an exercise.'
A fire in 1905 destroyed the whole of the top storey of the main building, along with the clock tower. Before the clock fell it struck 24 times.

Uppingham's Thring. Shrewsbury alone can fairly boast a unique triumvirate who, in the space of 110 years, turned a wreck of a school into one of exceptional scholarship, superlative location, and very high standing among the public schools of England.

As a result, there has very often been a tendency at Shrewsbury to view the reigns of Butler, Kennedy, and Moss as a long golden age. In the period 1864–7, Shrewsbury was sending on an estimated 50 per cent of its pupils to Oxford or Cambridge, and was, by that narrow criterion, the leading school in the country. In 1868, it was, as already described in detail, included among the 'Clarendon Seven'. But by 1902, towards the end of Moss's reign, things were rather different. One very detailed recent study, examining all schools, about 100 in all, with a claim to be called 'public schools' at that time, on a number of criteria, set Shrewsbury no higher than in the third grade of five; the twenty-two schools of Grade I are very much as one might expect, though the eight of Grade II might strike the observer as somewhat idiosyncratic; and the twenty of Grade III include a wide range. The criteria examined by the author include 'interaction' among schools; Oxford and Cambridge scholarship successes; the presentation of successful candidates to Oxford and Cambridge Higher Certificate Examinations; success in army entrance exams; and schools producing significant numbers of future Civil Service entrants. Shrewsbury does well only on the second and last of these criteria. (Salopians wounded in their pride may like to know that the author later concedes that a Grade II rating might be justifiable!)

For things were indeed far from perfect in the early years of the twentieth century. By 1909 numbers were at what was to prove their lowest level of the century – 240. Paradoxically, this must in part have been due to the move; it had not been welcomed by many Old Salopians, and, astonishingly, it is recorded that Alington on arrival at the school found only one boy – presumably G. E. Raven, himself the father and grandfather of Salopians – whose father had been a Salopian (this contrasts with a recent figure of about 18 per cent who are sons of Old Salopians). As one writer has put it, 'Masters come and go, and a returning Old Boy cannot bank on finding anyone still on the staff who taught him, so what he depends on are buildings and playing-fields which are identifiable with the sentimentalised memories of boyhood.'

When this is combined with the excessive length of Moss's tenure of office and the lure of entrance scholarships being instituted elsewhere which successfully channelled away some clever boys who might otherwise have naturally come to Shrewsbury, it is not surprising that the school's fortunes and standing had taken a marked turn for the worse before Alington arrived.

EXCURSUS
The Classics

Undoubtedly the most striking eulogy ever given to the influence of Shrewsbury or any other school on the study of the classics was that which appeared in a leading article in *The Times* in June 1932.

> Not the youngest boy or girl now learning Latin . . . but owes a debt, indirect perhaps but quite certainly traceable, to the old heroes of *Sabrinae Corolla*. Whether their names are as much honoured now as they used to be may be questioned, but there was nothing from the Psalms to a nursery rhyme that they could not turn into perfect hexameters or iambics; not a prize that they were not expected to carry off; not an honours list they were not expected to head. And it was like that for generations, and there has been nothing like it since. . . . The list could be prolonged indefinitely, while the ramifications of its spiritual descent would be beyond the powers of the most determined educational genealogist to map out. . . . What actual scholarship, and still more taste in literature generally, owes to Shrewsbury can never be accurately estimated; but it must be greater than is often recognized, even as Sabrina is probably the tributary least intelligible to the miscellaneous offspring of the Orontes now so freely permitted to participate in the stream of the nation's life.

W. Strang's 1914 portrait of Edward Branthwaite Moser, master 1875–1911 and 1915–1919, who gave his name to the library at the new site.

This tribute is due at least as much to Kennedy as to Butler (and much more than to his successor Moss), and it was in Kennedy's time that *Sabrinae Corolla* made its first appearance in 1850. But with the resignation of Moss in 1908 (he was not to die for another nine years) it is time to take a retrospective look at the achievements in classical scholarship of the previous 110 years. Moss's own pupils won University successes remarkable by any standards except those achieved under his immediate predecessors and the results achieved under the triumvirate fully justify the eulogy in *The Times* reprinted above. What can one say to 57 Browne Medals between 1806 and 1891? to 40 Porson Prizes between 1823 and 1892? to 15 Ireland or Craven Scholars at Oxford between 1827 and 1876?

Strang's portrait of Arthur Frederick Chance (also 1914), master 1880–1930. Chance's House became known as Forty The Schools for a reason which will be obvious to Latinists.

'The School breathed Greek', wrote Henry Woodd Nevinson, 'and through its ancient buildings a Greek wind blew. To enter Head Room – a dim, panelled chamber which the upper sixth used as a study – was to become a scholar. I doubt if good Greek verse could be written anywhere else. Winged iambics fluttered through the air; they hung like bats along the shelves, and the dust fell in Greek particles.'

Nevinson was a pupil under Moss, which may help to account for the rather jaundiced account which follows:

> Because Greek had been taught there for more than three centuries, they taught Greek. Of course we had Latin too, and up to the Sixth Form our time was equally divided between the two languages; but Latin, as being easier and rather more connected with modern life, never ranked so high, and we turned to it with the relief which most men feel when the ladies rise from the dinner-table. Latin prose, it is true, was accounted of more value than Greek prose, and no doubt there was some unrealised reason why. I suspect that in reality it is the more difficult; for it was the unconscious rule of our ancient tradition that of two subjects the more difficult was the better worth learning, provided always that both were entirely useless.
>
> Of Greek our knowledge was both peculiar and limited. We were allowed no devices to make the language in the least interesting – no designs, or pictures, or explanations. We had no idea what the Greek plays looked like on the stage, or why Demosthenes uttered those long-winded sentences. We knew nothing of the Dantesque underlying the tortured prose of Thucydides, and when a Sixth-Form master told us that the stupendous myth at the end of the *Phaedo* appeared to him singularly childish, we took no notice of the remark one way or the other. We only knew the passage was easy, just as Homer was easy, and a tragic chorus hard. The greater part of the school believed that Greek literature was written as a graduated series of problems for Shrewsbury boys to solve, and when a Sixth-Form boy was asked by a new master whether he did not consider the *Prometheus* a very beautiful play, he replied that he thought it contained too many weak caesuras.

Inevitably, the classical careers of most of those clever schoolboys ended with their Porsons and Irelands. But there were those who went on to make a real and enduring mark in the field of classical scholarship. Robert Scott, of Liddell and Scott's *Greek-English Lexicon*, has already been mentioned. H. A. J. Munro (who came in 1833), the first holder of the Professorship of Latin at Cambridge, produced a magisterial edition of Lucretius. J. E. B. Mayor (1938) succeeded Munro as Kennedy Professor; like Munro's Lucretius, Mayor's edition of Juvenal, eccentric as it is, retains some value today, a century after its publication. F. A. Paley's (1827) editions of Aeschylus and Euripides are still in use today: they are noteworthy for unassuming learning and great common sense. T. E. Page (1866) was for twenty-five years editor-in-chief of the Loeb Classical Library, a series the value of which only increases with the years (and the decline in minute knowledge of the classical tongues). I have written elsewhere that the nineteenth century was on the whole an undistinguished period for classical scholarship in England. This remains true (and a severe indictment by A. E. Housman has stood the test of time); but the

The Moss Gates, dedicated to 'Henrico Whitehead Moss', stand at the main entrance to the Schools. They were dedicated by Mrs Moss in 1923.

names appearing above made no small contribution to learning, while that of Munro is by any standard exceptional. Said Housman of Munro: 'In width and in minuteness of learning, in stability of judgment, and even in what is now the rarest of virtues, precision of thought, A. H. Palmer had superiors among his own countrymen and contemporaries; in some of these things many excelled him, some excelled him far, and Munro excelled him far in all.'

It will be sensible briefly to carry on this part of the story into the present century, when the classical tradition has been kept alive at the professional level by such men as A. J. B. Wace (1893), the excavator of Mycenae; Allan Blakeway (1912), who did much to revolutionise the study of early Greek history; E. A. Barber (1901), the editor of Propertius; and Maurice Platnauer (1901), the grammarian and metrician who edited plays of Euripides and Aristophanes. The many continuing successes of Old Salopians at Oxford and Cambridge are duly commemorated on the notice boards in the School Buildings; and it is proper to mention the name of J. L. Austin (1924), an Oxford classicist who was to become a Fellow of All Souls and a philosopher of great distinction (*Sense and Sensibilia*) before his untimely death in 1959.

In defiance of chronology, it seems useful to bring the story up to date.

At the conclusion of the Second World War, Shrewsbury was still decisively a 'Classical School'; in Michaelmas 1945 the Classical Upper Sixth was announced in the 'Brown Book' as being taught by

Mr Street and Mr Colman
assisted by
The Headmaster and Mr Dawson

In Michaelmas 1950, the twenty members of the Classical Upper Sixth still had two masters (Colman and Chenevix-Trench), and of those twenty, nine were to win open awards at Oxford or Cambridge; many University prizes, too, were won. In fact, however, things were not going to be the same; indeed, with the formation of a General Side in the late 1940s under Wolfenden, the almost automatic direction of boys to the Classical side must already have been marginally on the wane. Statistics can be dry things. But the following table shows starkly what in fact happened in the years that were to come:

Awards to Oxford and Cambridge,
and the decline of Classics

Decade	*Total*	*Classics*	*Classics as % of total*
1920–9	110	74	67
1930–9	96	53	55
1940–9	83	55	66
1950–9	99	38	38
1960–9	76	10	13
1970–9	91	14	15
Total	555	244	44

The evidence is incontrovertible; the long tradition, of which the Schools had been justifiably proud, was coming to an end. Classics has now become one subject among many and is, indeed, struggling to hold even its present attenuated position.

Already by 1963 the Head of Classics was having to say publicly that the classics were not dead, and that changes were in progress 'both in content and in organization by which they may elude ossification, petrification, and certain, if not sudden, death'. The curriculum was being made less specialized – no bad thing, when one realises that as late as 1951 it was possible in the Classical Sixth to devote twenty-six out of thirty school periods a week to the classics (if the Greek New Testament may be included); the other four periods went to English (three) and, typically, logic (one): no nonsense about science, nor had there been since School Certificate mathematics. The Head of Classics goes on to mention a Classical Society, the Agora, by which 'we, the sinister priesthood, want to build up a larger, better informed and *more sympathetic* laity' (my italics). Does one already sense a certain defensiveness? The article concludes by claiming that classics is 'distinctive in that it combines something of the logical precision of the Sciences with much of the humanism of, say, History or English' and that the author (W. B. Cook) could assure Old Salopians that 'we are fighting hard to preserve the classics here'. There is, perhaps, already just a hint of the last ditch.

Ten years later, Cook's successor as Head of Classics, A. J. Bowen, wrote about the changed status of Latin. Preparatory schools were not finding it easy to recruit classics teachers; Universities were changing their minds about Latin. The very young had become 'less literate, at least in the old grammatical way'. By that year (1973), just eleven boys a year on average were studying Latin to A level, and four Greek ('the position of Greek in preparatory schools is parlous indeed'). Bowen rightly added that 'no other subject has lost so much time at all levels. But that doesn't make classicists less intelligent than they were.' And it may be true that 'educationalists admit that no better test of general academic ability has ever been found than Latin.' Yet a Latin tag inevitably obtrudes itself: *Tempora mutantur, nos et mutamur in illis.* The school of Charles Darwin, if any school in the land, should know that one survives by evolution, and ultimately that is what has been happening. Pride in a noble tradition is justifiable; attempting to preserve a tradition artificially would not be. Shrewsbury is not mourning *les neiges d'antan.* After all, under Dr Kennedy 'French as a school subject was a mere figment . . . the hours supposed to be given to mathematics were too often spent in pleasant conversation, in the doing of impositions, that would otherwise have encroached upon our playtime, or sometimes in writing skits on subjects of school interest.' There is the other side of the sparkling coin of the golden era.

8

ALINGTON, SAWYER, HARDY

ALINGTON

WITH the arrival of Cyril Argentine Alington (1872–1955) as Headmaster in 1908, we seem to move at once into a significantly more modern era; an era of shorter headmasterships, of Headmasters coming from Oxford rather than one College, St John's, at Cambridge, and of a very gradual break with the classical tradition. Late in his life, Alington returned to Shrewsbury to preach, at the invitation of J. M. Peterson. For some reason Peterson had occasion to introduce me to the venerable Dean of Durham, and this soon emboldened me to send him a letter enquiring about some points of Salopian lore or history. As I write these words, his courteous and helpful letter of acknowledgement, in a spidery but scholarly and legible hand, lies on my desk, forming a link, however tenuous, with the past.

Alington, perhaps, is chiefly responsible for our gaining one of the few Honorary Old Salopians. . . .

C. A. Alington, headmaster 1908–1916, went from Shrewsbury to become headmaster of Eton. His relatively brief incumbency at Shrewsbury was, despite the war, one of exceptional activity and success. From the portrait by Fiddes Watt.

I sensed Alington as soon as I saw him walking the playing-fields at Shrewsbury, too handsome for any parson or pedagogue, with a longish face and a good jaw and quizzical eyes, and a twist to his mouth. He was tall and slender, with a slight stoop. Through the sunshine from the west he would walk over the cricket field from game to game, in his grey clericals. It was possible to play a dozen matches simultaneously at Shrewsbury, cheek by jowl, with cover-point in one engagement and square-leg in another back to back. A dozen matches flashing their white over the green; thuds of pursuing fieldsmen under your very nose; cricket balls whizzing through the air or volleying over the earth, menace to skull or shin. And Alington walked here and there, carrying his straw hat under his arm and chewing a daisy, the stalk in his mouth, with his black entanglement of wool called Bogey running ahead, a red tongue and nothing else telling you it was a dog. He moved like a man who saw and savoured himself as he moved. His voice fascinated me because of its suave inflections. One day I sat under the great cotton tree which dropped its white fleece on the field near the Chapel. I was reading Gilbert Murray's version of the *Medea* of Euripides, and Alington came by and stopped as he saw me; until now he had not spoken to me, except as one of the cricket professionals. He asked me what was my book; I told him, venturing at the same time one or two remarks (while my heart pounded away) in praise of the translation – and I knew not a word of Greek. Alington, in his most aromatic tones, gently said, 'Ah, yes, Murray is a most ingenious fellow.' It was my first living taste of irony. Irony in grey clericals at that! This was new to me. . . . Because of Alington, I call myself today an Old Salopian.

The staff in 1910. Headmaster C. A. Alington was, on his appointment, younger than all except two of his colleagues.

Alington appointed Shrewsbury's cricket professional, Neville Cardus, as his secretary in 1914. Cardus went on to publish some perhaps over-romantic accounts of Shrewsbury ('Shaftesbury') in his justly famed books on cricket. For all that, they seem to evoke memories of the golden summers before 1914, and his description of Shrewsbury's playing-fields as the 'most beautiful in the world' will not be denied – at least by Salopians.

Alington's headmastership, ended by his appointment to Eton, relatively brief as it was, and of course blighted by the outbreak of war, was one of important expansion. Numbers had been on a declining trend as Moss's reign drew to its close, and Alington inherited a school of about 240 boys. This had risen, war or no war, to 394 by the time he left; and rising numbers, allied to higher fees (£117 for a boarder against £90 at the end of the nineteenth century) and a certain amount of cunning (as when he persuaded Salopians to raise money via debentures to put up the Alington Hall), together with clever handling of the Governors, enabled an ambitious programme to go ahead.

But one of the most important elements of the programme was financed by a wholly different means, and the story shows how different still was a public school only eighty years ago from that of today. A new boarding House was needed. The Governors, as usual, were feeling hard up. Properties were already mortgaged. No suitable prospective conversion was to be found. As Michael Charlesworth relates, 'by parallel but separate approaches (Alington) got the Governors to agree that a House was necessary and he got J. B. Oldham [the only member of staff younger than himself] to write to the Governors agreeing to build a House, on stated conditions.' Lloyds Bank lent

Oldham the money – some £17,750, equivalent to something like half a million pounds today, originally at 4 per cent (implying equivalent interest payments of £20,000 a year). When Charlesworth asks 'what reception an individual schoolmaster would get today if he asked Lloyds Bank for half a million pounds to build a boarding house, without mortgage or guarantee', we may assume that the question is wholly rhetorical. The planning, appearance, and location of the House were alike successful, and the view from it across the Common was, until recently, one to give the eye much pleasure. Readers today, however, may not immediately spot the assumption underlying the financing: it was up to Housemasters to make what money they could from their charges – an old but bad system which was to change only with the arrival of Hardy in 1932. Not that Hardy was thanked for bringing about the change. Oldham would need to make a 'profit' of approximately £17 on each of his 42 boys just to meet the interest charges; this could not have been easy to do when a boy's total fees were less than £120 a year, and Oldham's natural generosity ensured that he was burdened with an overdraft for the rest of his long life.

It was also during the time of Alington that another building was put up with which Oldham was in due course to be almost permanently linked. The new library, or Moser Building, was completed in 1916 (and opened by a rather bored Cabinet Minister, Lord Milner). Other work led to the enlargement of the science buildings, chapel, and pavilion; the construction of a house (the 'New House') for bachelor masters; and the erection of a

The 1909 OTC band.

Watercolour painted by Bernard Gotch (1876–1936) in the early 1920s, showing 'Central' and the Alington Hall (1910) on the left. This was one of a series of illustrations of schools for a book which was never published.

The main school buildings: mid-Georgian in baroque dress, Sir Arthur Blomfield out of Thomas Pritchard.

H.B. WIMBUSH. 1891.

'temporary' armoury, still going strong, an object of derision to all, more than thirty years later. But one does not think of Alington as being primarily a 'building' Headmaster; thirty-five years old at the time of his appointment, a Marlburian, sometime scholar of Trinity College, and then Fellow of All Souls College, Oxford, he had been Master in College at Eton. His *Shrewsbury Fables*, his Latin *Carmen Salopiense* (1911), his later encouragement of the publication of *Two Men*, his wit and his facility at writing light verse – these are surely the signs of a man of letters rather than of one of action, and indeed he did much to widen the curriculum (introducing, for example, classes for the appreciation of art and music). Alington was the ideal Headmaster for a public school which needed the stimulus of a fresh brain and unimpaired energies; it was his good fortune to be Headmaster at a time which arguably represented the apogee of the 'public school ideal' (however one may wish to define or expand the term). But he also saw the outbreak of a war which was to take the lives of some 320 Old Salopians and those of five masters.

In *A Dean's Apology*, Alington writes: 'If it is not too much to say that the senior masters whom I found at Shrewsbury had literally given their lives to the school, the young men whom I was fortunate enough to appoint (at a miserably inadequate salary with no pension) were equally ready to identify themselves with it. I do not believe that it is senile optimism which makes me feel that there was about Shrewsbury in those days an extraordinary atmosphere.' Two of the masters were called Evelyn Southwell and Malcolm White, who came together as masters in 1910; they left together in 1915; and they met their deaths on the Somme in 1916. In 1919 there was published a remarkable book, *Two Men*, consisting of a memoir of them both, liberally illustrated by their correspondence. Inevitably, much of the book deals with their experiences as officers (and is all the more affecting because one knows

Opposite
Top: *Henry B. Wimbush's watercolour depicting the school regatta of 1891, the original for an engraving.*

Bottom: *Rowing on the Severn in 1989. The bank from the boathouse to the main buildings is even steeper than it appears in this photograph.*

The 1909 OTC. How many were still alive ten years later?

the end), though, since many of the letters are to Alington or other masters at Shrewsbury, the Schools make regular affectionate appearances. Four days before his death White wrote to Southwell to say 'Our New House and Shrewsbury are immortal, which is a great comfort'; and just before his own death Southwell in his diary thinks how 'a high wind on the Shropshire hills is good'. How was Alington feeling, as his young men went away to die? Ronald Knox, at a time of personal spiritual difficulty, had come to help out (and had become concerned lest he should be bound by Shrewsbury's 'golden chains', when he knew that his vocation would lead him elsewhere), and he may well have been a help. In his foreword to *Two Men*, Alington says 'The life of our Society from which they went was for those few years as nearly that of a happy family as any which the whole annals of schoolmastering can show.' They could have wished for no more eloquent epitaph.

As for Alington, let us speed him on his way to Eton with the help of Cardus:

> I saw *décor* in him, and irony. When he was appointed Headmaster of Eton, telegrams of congratulation were sent to him to Shrewsbury from all parts and from all ranks of society. He had them heaped like rose leaves in a bowl on the table of his library. He would come again and again into the room as the pile of *potpourri* grew from hour to hour, and he buried his hand in the orange envelopes and tissues and let them flutter like petals down to the bowl again. He could laugh at himself, and I think it is as well that all earnest young men should be brought into close and frank touch with somebody who *can* laugh at himself. Alington, I imagine, understood that the pride which is vain and goeth before a fall is one thing, and that æsthetic pride is another. I saw him as the artist who would be readier to interest himself in a boy's temperament than in the most successfully negotiated examination paper. He was, for me, an influence that inspired and corrected at one and the same time; not by precept but by example.

Alington's life was a long one; he was in his eighties when he died in 1955.

SAWYER

Harold Athelstone Parry Sawyer (1865–1939), Headmaster from 1917 to 1932, seems an unlikely figure for controversy: yet controversy there has been. He must have seemed a surprising, and perhaps unwelcome appointment, coming from St Bees, in his early fifties (the four previous Headmasters had averaged about twenty-nine on their arrival), with two second-class degrees from Oxford: a sharp contrast in every way to Alington, whose departure to Eton after only eight years, in the middle of a great war, may well have come as a surprise and disappointment to a staff several of whose members followed him south.

Tradition and anecdote have passed on the record of a man incompetent in small matters and indecisive in large. He must also, however, have been a man whom it was next to impossible to dislike. Sawyer's career at Shrewsbury began in a time of national crisis, and ended at another of world depression (and Salopian crisis). Yet it must speak volumes for the man, and his appointments to the staff, that the Schools' numbers rose from 394 to 517, or by over 30 per cent, during his headmastership. It was a period of some physical expansion, with the repurchases of Ridgemount in 1921 and of Severn Hill in the school year 1924–5. Then came the purchase of Kingsland House in 1930 (soon to be used as the Headmaster's residence – not the purpose for which it was bought), a building of some architectural distinction of which Thomas Telford may well have been the architect.

Not every term, not every year in a school's progress is marked by events of note: Sawyer's career at Shrewsbury ended with public successes and a private tragedy. The public successes included the visit in 1932 of the Prince of Wales to Kingsland to celebrate the jubilee of the move, and the winning of the Ladies' Plate at Henley for the second time (1924 was the first; only since Alington's day had the Schools sent a crew to Henley, and Alington was reported as saying that it had made him unpopular – at Eton!). More than fifty years have passed since, in Sawyer's last term as Headmaster, J. B. Oldham had to be asked to resign as Housemaster from the House which he had financed, designed, built, run, and jealously protected since 1911. What is known of the story – and it is unlikely that more will ever be known – is told, with great consideration and tact, in Michael Charlesworth's biography of Oldham, published in time for the House's seventy-fifth anniversary in 1986. Schoolmasters have been known both before and after to love not wisely but too well; Oldham's failing was well recognized by the Old Salopian who spoke generously about him at his memorial service in 1963, and it is good to recall that Oldham was to be allowed to give many more years' service to the school as its historian and Librarian, and was to achieve real distinction and widespread recognition as a bibliographer for his work on bindings. (Perhaps the story is not true: but the anecdote runs that S. S. Sopwith, then an assistant

A caricature of Canon Sawyer by Tom Purvis.

Severn Hill dates from the late eighteenth century; it was re-acquired by the school in 1924/5, having been earlier bought and sold in the 1890s.

The memorial at Severn Hill to Andrew Irvine, who died with Mallory at or near the summit of Mount Everest.

master, in Summer Term 1932, was asked to take over Oldham's Hall by Sawyer 'because Oldham had had a breakdown'. When the master pointed out that Oldham was to be seen proceeding normally about the Site, Sawyer replied, 'I mean, he's *going* to have a breakdown.')

A last familiar anecdote must be repeated. With Sawyer in the chair at a Masters' meeting, and with A. F. Chance at his elbow, S. S. Sopwith circulated a note:

> Chaos umpire sits
> And by decision more embroils the fray
> By which he reigns; next him, high arbiter,
> Chance governs all.

Perhaps, really, the quotation from Milton was thought of after the meeting; it remains no less apt.

HARDY

Henry Harrison Hardy (1882–1958), Headmaster from 1932 to 1944, was a man of a very different stamp; a Rugbeian, a layman (the first since Meighen in 1583), with a First Class in Classical Honour Moderations from New College, Oxford, Hardy was a Headmaster whose reputation has grown with the years. Appointed in his forties, he had already had high-level experience as Headmaster of Cheltenham. Changes were made. Hardy did not wish also to be Housemaster of School House (as one can now see, very sensibly so), and he moved into the recently acquired Kingsland House. Housemasters were no longer put in the position of needing to depend for part of their income on what they could make out of their flocks (and the profits lost by the Housemasters went into new buildings for the school). A regular full-time bursar was appointed (not before time, one may feel), as was a Director of Music and a Chaplain. The New Darwin Buildings were completed in 1938, following the gymnasium (1936); and the Housemasters' field had been acquired – originally by a group of masters and the bursar – as a shrewd tactical measure in 1934: it seems astonishing that the Governors could not or would not find the necessary sum, just £1,000. The field was ultimately sold (with the retention of important safeguards) for £50,000 in 1979.

Wrote J. B. C. Grundy, himself a future Headmaster, in a shrewd and not unsympathetic study, of Hardy's methods:

> Salopians, never unduly punctilious about time, now found themselves working to the twenty-four-hour clock; official notices had numbered paragraphs like operation orders; at OTC inspections the headmaster accompanied the visiting general not in top hat and tails, as Bob (Sawyer) had done, but in a well-worn khaki. Long hair, to which the Shrewsbury boys were prone half a century before the Beatles, was now tabooed. The new headmaster rode to first lesson at 7.45 a.m. in cap and gown upon a tall bicycle and, it was whispered, *across the first eleven wicket*. No doubt he did so only in dry weather in one of the winter terms, but it was a blasphemy.
>
> Hardy had, it seemed to me, all the virtues and some of the limitations of a British

The school wall, moved from the Old Schools in 1884. The wall had several locations at Kingsland before reaching its final resting place, parallel to 'Central', in 1932. The qualifications for having one's name inserted have inevitably become more rigorous over the years.

> classical education. Endowed with a most accurate memory, a wide experience and an influential circle of acquaintances, he was apt to hold a precedent intrinsically superior to an argument, an antecedent more valuable than a qualification. Where crafty Bob had thrown up his hands and left a problem to the housemasters, Hardy could cite the solution of it at Rugby or Winchester twenty years before, and often enough it was the sounder course – but it had not evolved locally.

Hardy was not generally popular; when I came as a new boy to the Schools in 1945, a year after his departure, his nickname 'Hitler' was still prevalent. Indeed, he had not had an easy time of it, inheriting as he did an elderly staff, perhaps too accustomed to having their own way. Even D. J. V. Bevan, kindest of men, and a master but not (yet) a Housemaster under Hardy, has conceded that malice towards Hardy may not have been 'wholly lacking'. The diversion of Kingsland House from its intended purpose as a boarding house cannot have been popular; nor was the introduction of regular PT on Central, the approach to the main school buildings from the main school-gates, a planned revolt by the boys having to be nipped in the bud by the Head of School and praepostors.

That he was capable of great efficiency is shown, almost unintentionally, by Richard Cobb in *A Classical Education*. Not all Salopians are of saintly or even good disposition, and Cobb was the contemporary and close friend of another former member of Rigg's who, in 1936, committed matricide. Cobb's account, understandably looking at matters from his own standpoint, yet shows that Hardy not only made a special visit to talk matters over with him in London (Cobb by now being up at Oxford), but, by using his widely ranging influence, managed to keep the name of Shrewsbury entirely out of the newspapers. Earlier in this narrative there appeared some extracts from John Coker Egerton's diary. We also happen to possess another set of diaries, by a Ridgemount boy, W. F. Ewbank (1931–6). Their interest, paradoxically, lies in their very ordinariness: work, games, out-of-school activities, the 'Corps' – all are described with placid good humour. Hardy is mentioned fairly often, with 'Hitler' alternating with the surname and an occasional 'Headman'; but there is no perceptible animus in the published excerpts, as Ewbank worked his way up to becoming Head of House; indeed, it would be hard to say what attitude, if any, the diarist had towards the Headmaster – perhaps a healthy sign. To return to Cobb, he has given the world, in *A Sense of Place*, some highly coloured accounts of life at Shrewsbury in the 1930s (with which at least one of his near-contemporaries would not agree); but two comments about Hardy have a ring of truth: 'The Headmaster also helped to make me appreciate the splendid language of the Old Testament, as well as the beauty of the Shropshire hills. Under rather a severe exterior, he was a kindly, compassionate man who, during the War, took infinite trouble to keep up with former members of the school who were serving in the Forces.' The other story is, to me, simply funny: 'Subsequently, Clover was beaten by the Headmaster for having written for every answer in the Certificate "A" examination "Dig a latrine". (Question: You are about to order your platoon over the top. What do you tell your men? Answer: Dig a latrine.)' Hardy was fully justified, if perhaps a little lacking in humour. Cobb gives affectionate pen-sketches of those masters he liked ('Kek' McEachran, S. S. Sopwith, R. H. J. Brooke, Frank Macarthy, above all J. R. M. Senior), but does not refrain from dealing with others, including his Housemaster, with great severity: he who runs may read, and at least some of his views (for and against) were shared by Kyffin Williams in his *Across the Straits*.

If one were now to decide who was to become the most widely known Old Salopian of those years, it would arguably be one who, at school was 'morose and silent', a non-co-operator, seldom smiling, always standing on his own in tacit disapproval of his schoolfellows. Richard Hillary, author of *The Last Enemy*, was in Churchill's, under J. O. Whitfield (1931–7), though he makes hardly any mention of Shrewsbury in the book which made his name. It has to be said that by no means everybody was charmed by him and if the following, admittedly funny, story about him is true, it is not difficult to see why. It comes from Ronald 'Scott Thorn's' autobiography, *Star Doctor.* '

> Richard Hillary, Battle of Britain fighter ace and war hero, was [Whitfield's] chief tormentor. Hillary used to run back to the house after First Lesson at 7.30, steal J. O. Whitfield's copy of *The Times* and read it nonchalantly in the dining hall at breakfast. Eventually, JOW would come in breathing heavily from the exertion of the same journey from the school buildings.
>
> 'Hillary!' he gasped.
>
> 'Yes, sir?' Hillary replied continuing to read imperturbably.

'You've taken my *Times*: give it me back.'

'When I've finished it. Certainly sir.'

There followed an explosion inside JOW's throat and chest but he was beyond protest. He backed out defeated, making incoherent noises.

But Hillary was a very special case, as he later proved, and when in his final year JOW made one of his rare rounds of food enquiries he asked Hillary if there was anything wrong with his boiled egg.

'Yes,' replied Hillary. 'It's rock hard, I suspect rotten and quite inedible.'

To demonstrate his points, he took the egg and threw it the length of the hall. It struck the wall above Matron's ducking head and dislodged a piece of plaster the size of a dinner plate. This in turn loosened the support of a large picture of a former housemaster, which crashed to the floor with the unmistakable sound of breaking glass.

'You . . . you . . . unutterable vandal,' spluttered JOW. 'Your father will get a bill for all that immediately.'

Hillary pressed his attack in the same ruthless way that I imagine he dealt with several Messerschmitts. Smiling he said,

'My father's broke, sir.'

(Here let it be said that this story is far more revealing of Hillary than of Whitfield; anybody who knew that formidable man and Housemaster may well suspect that the anecdote gained much with the passage of nearly half a century, and may well include an element of wish-fulfilment. Even ten years later, when Whitfield was no longer a Housemaster, he was by no means a man to trifle with. If 'Scott Thorn's' narrative could be taken *au pied de la lettre*, one must suspect that the punishment visited upon Hillary would have been swift and condign. It has to be added that, in the course of working on this book, I have encountered many Salopian stories which, however apposite, amusing, or revelatory in themselves, strain credulity up to and beyond its limits. On Hillary's character, there is independent evidence enough; and one may reasonably doubt whether amiability was the first attribute to be looked for in a fighter pilot.)

It was Hardy's lot to be Headmaster when war came in 1939. Almost at once, his former school Cheltenham was 'billeted' on Shrewsbury (as it happened, only for two terms). Great resourcefulness was necessary, and was forthcoming. The Salopian *Newsletter* in 1980 published an admirable account by a Cheltonian which is reproduced below:

It was just 40 years ago that Cheltenham College returned to their own site after their war time evacuation to Shrewsbury which lasted for two terms, Michaelmas 1939 and Lent 1940. Their buildings were requisitioned and they found themselves homeless within a fortnight of the start of the September term. H. H. Hardy, himself a former headmaster of Cheltenham, invited them to Shrewsbury where they moved into billets and shared the Site with Salopians – one of the most extraordinary periods in the history of either school. We reproduce an article written by one of the Cheltenham evacuees which was published in the *Cheltonian* and also in *Country Life*.

'If all goes well the beginning of April will see the end of one of the adventures in co-operation which the exigencies of war have forced upon many public schools. Cheltenham College will be returning to Cheltenham for its summer term after having been for two whole terms the guests of Shrewsbury.

Guests in a sense. It is no fault of Shrewsbury that it has been a queer sort of hospitality. When one asks people to stay one generally offers them a spare room. In a school, however, there are few spare rooms, and particularly is this so in a school in such a thriving condition as Shrewsbury. In the science laboratories advanced practical work has been done by members of both schools at the same time, but otherwise all that could be arranged was to offer Cheltenham the use of rooms and teaching equipment at times when Shrewsbury masters were not in occupation. The time-tables of both schools had to be adjusted, and the result was some very neat pieces of dovetailing. If Cheltenham boys were handed out rather large slabs of afternoon work, they took them without complaint. It was obvious that Shrewsbury's normal routine must be disturbed as little as possible.

Besides, the Cheltenham time-table had attractive compensations. Boys might be called to school from the lunch table every afternoon of the week but one, but most of the morning was theirs instead, and in the fogs of November and the black-out of later months those morning hours that gave them a monopoly of the sun were very good value indeed.

In descriptions of this and other school evacuation arrangements there have been too many references to Box and Cox. These two gentlemen, one seems to remember, were kept apart by the mercenary wiles of their landlady. But here in Shrewsbury, on the famous Kingsland 'Site' – surely the most beautiful of all public school settings – it is Box that has entertained Cox.

Box has given up some of his most cherished preserves so as to make life easier for Cox. The entire upper floor of the boat-house has been made over to Cheltenham's bursar for offices and school bookshop. The major portion of the cricket pavilion has been converted into a common room for the Cheltenham staff. The Alington Hall – Shrewsbury's central meeting hall – has been relinquished for the duration of Cheltenham's stay. This became immediately the hub of their world, a corner of the site that looked in the early days as if it might be for ever Cheltenham. For when the College's entire movable effects (other than personnel) arrived in sixteen railway containers shortly before the beginning of the autumn term, it was here that they were dumped, for subsequent distribution to billets.

Later the Alington Hall became Cheltenham's main place of assembly. Here every morning before Chapel the whole College meets for the daily barrage of notices and instructions. It is a time of great activity for house-masters and house captains, for here they are with their houses in rows beside them, and unless a house meeting is expressly ordered later in the day this gathering-in of the flock will not occur again till next morning's 'assembly'.

That is one of the problems of Cheltenham's present existence, and the main reason, one imagines, why a great shout of joy went up when it was given out in assembly that the Government were giving them back their buildings in May. Life in billets may be amusing. It may be interesting. There are stories of boys being brought early morning cups of tea, of a hushed but forceful whisper on the stairs, overhead by a delighted billeter: 'If you wake that baby again tonight, I'll kill you.' But no collection of billets, however close together, however luxurious, however *bizarre*, can offer compensation for the corporate life of a College house. For what compensation could there be, other than the house itself?

Some, if not all of their College's houses Cheltenham is getting back for the summer term. It does not yet know its precise fate. Its main buildings, swept and garnished and elaborately black-curtained, but as empty of humanity as so many gasometers, are, we understand, also to be restored to their normal uses. All this must be some consolation to Cheltenham for what the last six months has brought them: this, and the feeling that, even if their exile has not assisted materially in the active prosecution of the war, the burden of some ultra-responsible brows may have been lessened by the thought of those buildings standing ready in case of need.

Other consolations there have been, too. There was the twofold Armistice Day victory on the common, Shrewsbury's main playing-field. In the morning the Shrewsbury Soccer XI defeated Bradfield, and in the afternoon the Cheltenham Rugby XV defeated Rugby. In honour of the double event enough school periods were sacrificed to enable each school to watch the other's game. As *The Times* commented later in a leading article: 'The normal advantage of the home side must have been enhanced by a double storm of thunder, for we cannot doubt that Cheltenham shouted for Shrewsbury, Shrewsbury for Cheltenham. There is one blasphemous speculation which will obtrude itself. Did any Salopian allow himself to whisper that perhaps Rugby was the more exciting game of the two? Was there a Cheltonian with soul so dead as to fancy for one regretful moment that Association was better suited to his own individual talents?'

The Times, 'in a spirit of sturdy conservatism,' hoped not. And with *The Times* we must hope that 'the most wide-minded admission made was that the other fellow's was not a bad game.'

Floods in March 1940 when thaw followed the great frost.

Shrewsbury's invitation to Cheltenham to join in the Tucks run made another pleasant piece of history. Running at Shrewsbury has a ritual of its own. It has always been organized as a Hunt; its officials are Huntsmen, Senior and Junior Whips, and Gentlemen of the Runs. Record or 'Hound' Books of the runs exist in an unbroken series from 1842. The Tucks, originally named after the farmer from whose farm it started, used to be compulsory for the whole school, for the simple reason that it was held on the day of Shrewsbury races by more than a mere coincidence. Nearly all the school still take part in it, and this year by Cheltenham's acceptance of the Huntsman's invitation, the pack swelled to the record number of three hundred and forty-two couples.

There were consolations even in the Arctic conditions that greeted the two schools on their return in January. On the first Sunday of Shrewsbury's term the thermometer fell to minus 6 °F. (official: Shrewsbury Meteorological Office). A few days later a thaw set in which broke up the ice on the Severn just about the time when Cheltonians were arriving back. There was to be no more skating on the Severn, but the previous heavy falls of snow had left plenty of flood-water on the common, and there were two good spells of skating there later, within a stone's throw of the School buildings, the baths, the gymnasium, and the shop. How many other schools had their ice-rink brought to their door like this? Not a few, one hopes. For here on Kingsland it made at any rate the skaters among us – and their name was legion – put up contentedly with long trudges home in slush to houses where the water gushed from the walls or descended like a gentle rainstorm from the ceiling but seldom if ever could be made to emerge from the end of a tap.

One of the great merits of our little ice age was that it brought the ordinary inconspicuous Cheltonian and Salopian together unselfconsciously. Members of the debating and other learned societies have met formally on many occasions. But here on the ice on Sunday afternoons and in gaps in the dovetailing on other days, preparatory school and home friendships could be casually happily renewed. There was, too, a famous ice hockey match between Cheltenham and Shrewsbury – yet another unique event for the two schools' annalists to prize.

To non-skaters Shrewsbury offered a toboggan run, down the cliff-like bank from the Site to the Severn. Of this the writer, who tried it out, can only say that those who did will now be able to face the Grand National and the Cresta Run, and the Kingston by-pass on August Bank Holiday, without a qualm. Shrewsbury earned the eternal gratitude of Cheltenham by providing most of the toboggans.

They were in a way repaying a debt, for Cheltenham had lent Shrewsbury upwards of a hundred bicycles for one of their country excursion holidays last term. Life for Cheltenham would be difficult indeed without bicycles. Most of the College billets are a matter of a few minutes only from the school buildings, thanks to the bicycle, but there are a few so deep in the wilds of the country that, so the story goes, when a boy was ill recently his temperature had to be taken with a horse thermometer, none other being available.

In the old days, to judge by the stories they have inspired, if two schools had been thrown into such provocative proximity there would certainly have been fights. The only inter-school fight that has occurred so far was an extremely elaborate and well-ordered affair. The venue was the deer park at Attingham, and the chief weapons rifles and bren guns. A bridge was bombed by an aeroplane said to belong to Cheltenham. Heavy loss of life was reported, but all ended happily with both school bands playing the column home; and, as the official report puts it, 'much valuable experience was gained'.

> 'Much valuable experience gained.' Whether it has been on the river in Shrewsbury's tubs and clinker fours, or on the Wrekin on the ubiquitous push-bike, or getting the Sunday lunch fire ready in the shelter of the Stiperstones, or spinning for pike at Atcham; wherever Providence and a map have taken this boy or that, this must be the ultimate consolation, to fortify Cheltenham for their return to their own loved haunts.'

David Bevan, writing after Hardy's death in 1958, gives full credit to Hardy as being 'assured a place among the great headmasters'; and when one bears in mind the grave burdens under which he laboured from 1939 to 1944 (though numbers, all things considered, kept up remarkably well: they were as high as 465 in 1944 and 488 in 1945, with Shrewsbury's relative security from bombing and V1 and V2 raids perhaps being a marginally positive factor) the praise seems justified. Certain it is that his reputation has grown with the years; and if he had to live down a deserved reputation for authoritarianism in his early days at the school, he did so with success under the least enviable of circumstances; and the lot of a Headmaster who introduces needed tightening-up and reform is never likely to prove a popular one. Reform or even response to a need can seem like reproach, and tact and presentation were not always Hardy's strong points (not charges that could ever be laid against his gentle, highly popular, and even widely loved wife). It was Hardy's son, the actor Robert Hardy, who came to open the school's new theatre in 1984 – converted from his father's gymnasium of 1936. Shrewsbury was again fortunate in her second Rugbeian Headmaster.

9

FROM WOLFENDEN TO THE PRESENT

WOLFENDEN

J. F. WOLFENDEN (later Sir John, and finally Lord Wolfenden) spent only six years of his long life – born in 1906, he died in 1985 – at Shrewsbury. Another Oxford man, who had been a philosophy don at Magdalen, then appointed Headmaster of Uppingham at only twenty-seven, he was still relatively young when he came to Shrewsbury in 1944. We have an account of those years from his own pen in *Turning Points*, his disappointingly bland autobiography. From it one gains the impression that he and the school always stood at a slight distance from one another, a situation physically aggravated by the noticeable distance of Kingsland House from the central action of the Schools.

John Frederick Wolfenden, headmaster 1944–1950. Successful as a headmaster, J. F. (later Lord) Wolfenden perhaps remains best known for his chairmanship of the Commission on Homosexuality and Prostitution, and his distinguished career in public life. The portrait in the Alington Hall is by Peter Inchbald.

They were times of difficulty, with the early years of peace being scarcely less difficult, indeed in some ways more difficult, than those of war. Older staff members needed to be replaced; other, younger ones wanted to be accommodated again upon their return from service in the Forces. Numbers almost at once began to fall, if not quite as seriously as has sometimes been implied; by 1948 they had fallen by 26 to 462, compared with 1945 (representing a total loss in revenue of about £4,000 per annum). Whether this was the Schools' 'fault' may be doubted; Southern schools had become safe again, and transport difficulties, with virtually no petrol available, were not negligible. Money was, as so often, hard to come by, and there was to be almost no new building of significance until the 1960s. Of course, there was excellent teaching in many subjects, scholarships were still being won, and a strong games tradition was being maintained. I have already written in the Salopian *Newsletter* about what it was like then to be a boy at Shrewsbury. As it may help to give something of the flavour of the times, here is part of my article again:

> Laurence Le Quesne's admirable article about the changing face of the Site has prompted these random recollections from one who, with about a hundred others, became a new boy ('new scum') at Shrewsbury in Michaelmas 1945, when a Salopian's *life* was also very different from what it is now (1987). The term began, by the way, on September 25th.
>
> The date gives a clue. The Second World War had ended only a month or so before our arrival, and the school in many ways was still operating under wartime conditions. Most obvious, I suppose, was the virtually compulsory enrolment in the

JTC (later CCF), with its twice-weekly parades, regular Field Days, and an annual, and highly unpopular, week in camp – typically at Rhyl in early August. Then there was the Home Farm, or allotments, near Ridgemount – not impinging on the lives of most of us. There was, inevitably, a staff with a high percentage of masters who had nobly had to soldier on scholastically while others were doing real soldiering: many would soon retire or be replaced by Wolfenden's long stream of new appointments that included Michael Charlesworth and Tony Chenevix-Trench.

But this was not the sort of thing that a new boy noticed, with the Brown Book to read, his Colour Exam to prepare for, the douling to be carried out, Hall Elections, the unaccustomed sound of First Bell, the hundreds (seemingly) of practices and customs to be learned about – and emphatically *not* practised. (Luckily for me, it was a kindly House Monitor who told me not to leave my tweed jacket undone.) Even more immediate were the shortages – at one time, for example, gym shoes were virtually unobtainable, which was tiresome when one had to do six 'changes' every week. Fives balls were so hard to come by that the Captain of Fives was reduced to advertising for them in *The Salopian*: one had to play with objects in the last state of decrepitude, stuck together with Sellotape. Electricity would fail unexpectedly, not that we minded *that*, when it happened in form. In winter, we were always cold; above all, throughout the year, we were hungry, despite the best efforts of a Housemaster still equipped with a sizable domestic staff (including House John). It must have been dispiriting for him to watch the massed sprint of boys after house lunch to the School Shop – but we at Oldham's, coarse souls, were thinking only 'we should get there ahead of Ridgemount and Severn Hill'. These shortages were soon to be exacerbated by the appalling winters of 1945–6 and

The last night of the Bumpers 1949; the author, at the right in cricket flannels, is looking at the camera.

1946–7 – well photographed in *The Salopian* of the time, with the waters of the Severn almost lapping, it seemed, St Chad's. And there were other, less obvious shortages which one can only see with the benefit of hindsight and the passage of time: the privilege of going down town was rationed (not that there was much to do, buy, or eat, especially with Sidoli's being out of bounds), and entertainments were few and far between.

The Shrewsbury of 1945 was in essence that of 1939, as so splendidly displayed in Martin Adie's video-film of the late 1930s. Never mind Oliver's Egg, the Smokers, the Pier, the Armoury, the uninterrupted view from Oldham's across the Common: what matters lies in the attitudes, still utterly conformist and hierarchical (from the new boy, the one-year-old, the two-year-old, etc. up to the Praepostor with his walking-stick, and the brusher whom one capped); the clothing (blue suit, with white shirt and stiff collar, on Sundays); the assumptions (up to three chapel services and a Divinity Lesson on Sundays – though at least the Divinity Lesson did not last long after 1945); the relatively large idiosyncratic vocabulary (skytes, tweak, wazz, basher, dixbarn, Benjie's); the supremacy of the classics (the Sidney Gold Medal, the Moss Prize, the liberal presence of Greek in *The Salopian*); the rigid stratification between years, Houses, subjects; and let it be admitted (in those days before easy travel, of petrol rationing and exchange controls) perhaps there was a certain blinkered, even philistine, approach to the world on the part of most of us youthful public schoolboys, who yet called ourselves 'men'. In those first years after the war we at Shrewsbury, who automatically lined the football pitch on Senior whenever we were playing Malvern, Repton, or Charterhouse – were we, perhaps, among the last inheritors of the public school tradition as exemplified elsewhere by Arnold and Thring, at Shrewsbury by Butler, Kennedy, and Moss? Perhaps so, but we assuredly did not know it, as we unquestioningly accepted gating and Top Schools, beating and being beaten, douling and capping, rules, restrictions, traditions and customs without number. I suspect that if we, in the late 1940s, had been cast back by a time-warp to the Shrewsbury of the first decade of the 1900s, we should have found it a lot less strange than today's Salopian if he could be thrown back to the 1940s. All the same, however bitter on occasion the vintage, perhaps we had the last of the wine.

Extraordinary entrepreneurship was shown by a boy in Ingram's who, with devoted care, great ingenuity, remarkable resources and resourcefulness, and other qualities which should have marked him out as a leader among men, actually constructed a fully furnished and lavishly equipped study for himself (and selected cronies) *under* the floor of another study in the House. The project was believed to have taken years, with the displaced earth being added to that of the House allotment. Admittedly, the Housemaster had been at a loss to account for intermittent mysterious fusings of the electricity supply, but he had got no further. When it was all accidentally discovered in Michaelmas 1945 by the Head of House, the boy had to go, but admiration for his achievement was not limited to those few who were privileged to see the study in question. A more dangerous breach of discipline occurred a year or two later, with the discovery of the theft of live ammunition from one of the dumps in the district. Wolfenden, in the Alington Hall, called for a full confession from the miscreants, promising (if memory serves) an amnesty if all explosive material were handed in. Wolfenden handled this potentially grave affair with aplomb. But I have already observed that not all Salopians are saints, and another boy of Wolfenden's time later achieved the melancholy distinction of being murdered by Ruth Ellis, the last woman to be hanged in Britain. It has to be said that he was not a pleasant person, and was later accurately portrayed in a successful film, *Dance with a Stranger*.

Wolfenden limited his teaching, but taught the Classical Sixth at least some elements of philosophy, a subject which he had taught at a much higher level at Oxford; and, twice Chairman of the Headmasters' Conference, he steadily became well known at a national rather than only a local level: indeed, when he left the school at the time of the production of a 'musical extravaganza' called *The 'Postors of Romance*, the line 'they'll miss him on the London train' raised a roar of laughter from the entire school.

He went on to make a considerable impact elsewhere: Vice-Chancellor of Reading University, Chairman of the Committee which produced the Wolfenden Report on Homosexuality and Prostitution, Chairman of the University Grants Committee, Director of the British Museum, he had a career that was successful by any standards except, perhaps, his own. In the smaller world of Shrewsbury, he made some twenty staff appointments, of whom half stayed until they retired, and several others became Headmasters elsewhere, notably Anthony Chenevix-Trench at Bradfield, Eton, and Fettes. If not all his appointments were successful, that would be statistically predictable; certainly several were to prove not only successful but highly influential, at Shrewsbury and elsewhere. His own estimation of his stay at Shrewsbury is too modest:

> I felt that somehow I had never made much impact on Shrewsbury. I do not think that there was any conscious resistance: certainly there was no overt opposition. But Shrewsbury in those days was the kind of school which could to all intents and purposes – or at least to all outward appearance – have got on quite cheerfully without any Headmaster at all. . . . There never seemed to be much of what they call a 'challenge'. . . . One explanation might be that the place was so settled in its ways that it would never accept that anybody had changed it; another is that it is possible to do good by stealth.

This is too dismissive by far. His impact was indeed felt throughout the school, and his obituarist in the *Newsletter* paints a picture that is much more recognizable to one who spent five years as a boy under him at Shrewsbury:

> It is difficult now to recreate the world of the last year of the war. There was certainly some weight behind the 'highly competent body of masters'; the Housemasters were Hope-Simpson, Pendlebury, Street, Taylor, Phillips, Tombling, Sale, Sopwith and Bevan. All except Taylor and Bevan had held their Houses for some time. Yet looking down the Brown Book there were ten masters away at the war and twelve temporary appointments, mostly of older men headed by the venerable John Key. In the next six years Wolfenden was to appoint seven new Housemasters and no less than 20 new members of the staff – exactly half the 1950 total. It was here that he made a very significant and lasting contribution to Shrewsbury, though there is hardly a mention of this in his book.

History Side in the early 1950s, in the room where Moss taught the Sixth.

He was aware too of the 'royal and ancient thread' running through the fabric. He saw the importance of Philip Sidney as a symbol; he appreciated the heritage of Butler, Kennedy, and Moss; it was he who persuaded Alington to pay his first visit to the School for many years; he who first invited the Mayor and Corporation to visit the Site with due ceremonial. And, in the post-war years, he keenly encouraged Old Salopians to revisit the Site, not least General Sir Miles Dempsey, the outstanding Salopian soldier of the Second World War. In material matters these were not easy days; rationing continued for the whole of his headmastership. The future of public schools was uncertain. The astronomical rise of fees frightened everybody. It is not always appreciated that the fee of £180 per annum charged in 1945 was unchanged from the 1920 figure. Now in Wolfenden's day the fee went up to £251. Numbers actually slightly declined in these years and were far short of the 1939 figure. Nor was it possible to do much to refurbish the buildings, still less to expand facilities, with permits and quotas and shortages of every type of material.

But if material matters were difficult and post-war Britain was gloomy, yet the rise in general morale at Shrewsbury was very marked indeed. It was partly of course that senior boys now expected to live and not die, partly that so many younger faces were appearing on the staff. But mainly because in JFW there was a real leader, energetic, active, interested, carrying with him a sense of purpose which penetrated all sides of school life. From the Head of School to the school porter, life was full of interest and incident. There was a radical reform of the curriculum, long overdue. Those who laboured through the plethora of IVth and Vth and Remove forms on the endless ladder up the school will remember that old system without affection. Now it was streamlined. New examinations were meaning revised syllabuses. New staff meant new methods of teaching. But Wolfenden's influence was not felt only in reorganization. Praepostors' meetings were instituted at which it seemed the boys themselves (in their own estimation) were taking a major part in steering the ship of state. On Monday mornings in the Alington Hall the whole school was gathered and the Headmaster commented, directed, criticized, or praised. On the rare occasions when, after prayers, he dismissed the school without saying anything there was an almost audible sigh of disappointment. Masters' meetings, held at 9.15 p.m. after prayers in Houses, had full agendas which ranged from House socks to education on the highest possible level and what-I-said-to-the-Minister. And these were proper meetings; gowns were worn, no casual smoking, no creeping in late nor disappearing early.

The wonder is that a man who was so often away could keep so tight a hold on every aspect of school life; and he had time – time for the worries of junior boys, time for a chat with newly appointed masters, time to entertain in the happy domestic circumstances of Kingsland House where Eileen kept so hospitable a home amongst her young children. Some may recollect the rather gaunt figure standing at the window of the School House study at 7.45 a.m. to see who was late for 1st Lesson, he having returned from London by the midnight train and having already done an hour's work on his postbag. His lunch time routine was studied. In those days there was 'after 12', that useful hour before lunch. JFW, his morning's work completed by one o'clock, wearing his mortar board as ever, would walk home to Kingsland House taking a quarter of an hour to do so, walking round the fives courts in winter, spending time at the cricket nets in summer, talking to perhaps twenty boys *en route*, seeing and being seen. He believed in keeping in touch.

In the varied and extensive panorama of his public life, Shrewsbury in retrospect seems but a brief episode. Some have spoken somewhat slightingly of his Shrewsbury years – 'just a step on the ladder'. And to some – and Old Salopians among them – he never seemed to have his heart in a place which he left so often. Not always did he strike a sympathetic note with those whose conception of headmastering was founded on the Alington–Sawyer years. Was he too clever by half? Was his remarkable intellectual speed and incisiveness too much for the slower and duller? Did a certain irritation creep in too readily when there were fools to suffer and his carefully prepared plans were upset? The manner of his resignation provides a good example. He had made very careful plans that all should know of his going at the same moment – letters to parents posted, staff informed, press release, etc. The news was announced to the staff at a late night meeting and the boys were to be informed in the Alington Hall after 1st Lesson. The bombshell was duly dropped to the staff, whereupon a master said, 'The boys already know.' JFW was rather more than put out. That evening the Forum Society had visited the works of the *Shrewsbury Chronicle* and seen the announcement being set up. 'The Society studies current affairs,' said the master in charge; it didn't help. Wolfenden did not like any departure from the script – his script.

He had his little weaknesses. Yet Shrewsbury owes him much. His influence and example counted enormously in those post-war years, however much he may have discounted them and no Salopian of that time will look back otherwise than with respect and admiration, glad to have encountered even briefly one of such exceptional endowments wedded to a liberal and urbane spirit founded in the philosophy don which he never quite failed to be. He was recognized as the best Committee Chairman of his generation, and on speech days, prize giving and educational occasions he was without peer. His powers in both these spheres were displayed and appreciated during his time on the Site.

In his address at his Memorial Service, the Dean of Guildford recorded an anecdote. On a Hellenic Cruise the Dean was swimming in the ship's pool when Jack Wolfenden came by, formally dressed as ever in a pin-stripe suit wearing a hat. 'Come and swim, Jack!'. 'I never take off my clothes in public', was the reply. It was more than a sartorial comment. Though a very public man he remained a very private person.

Wolfenden was keen on tradition – he was credited with announcing that 'starting today, there will be a tradition of such-and-such', but did he really intend to reintroduce straw boaters, known as 'bashers'? Here is what two well-known Salopians had to say about the idea in the lively pages of *The Salopian* early in 1946:

> Dear Sir,
> A little dicky-bird has told us that 'bashers' are about to be reintroduced. There are, we know, some few reasons why this should be so, including their use as a target for air-gun pellets, but there are more why it should not. The expense of this kind of headwear is seldom taken into account, but we can tell you they are not given us free. The fact that in the year dot, X misbehaved himself in Shrewsbury is no reason why we should wear dustbin lids on our heads. I suppose it is a tradition that they should be around, but aren't we just the teeniest weeniest bit tired of that word? From the æsthetic point of view, their outline is similar to a gasometer, their texture not far off that of a cowshed in winter, their detail and decoration either non-existent or lurid, and their colour a nondescript pale yellow. In short, the impression they give is that of a nigger minstrel who does not know any better. Are they really necessary?
>
> Yours, etc.,
> J. C. Nottingham
> W. E. Court

It is a fair guess that, as he read those words, Wolfenden would have smiled. At all events, and for whatever reason, no more was heard of 'bashers'; and John Nottingham went on to become Head of School. And a sign of the times: in the adjoining column, a correspondent was pleading for the institution of a 'General Side'. Within a very few years he had his wish.

PETERSON

John Magnus Peterson (1902–78) who succeeded Wolfenden in 1950 (being, incidentally, the older by some four years) shared with his predecessor a First in Greats as well as great ability at games, Peterson's speciality being Eton fives and Wolfenden's hockey, at which he had been an international. The resemblance ended there. To start with, Peterson was himself an Old Salopian, who had been Head of School, and it seemed fitting that an OS Headmaster – who was also the outstanding candidate – should preside over the fourth centenary celebrations, due to take place in 1952. Again, while Wolfenden had happily occupied Kingsland House in the company of a wife and young family, Peterson had had to endure the death of his own much-loved wife while he was a housemaster at Eton, and it seemed that he had not recovered from the loss. Wolfenden was an unashamedly ambitious man, the reverse of the generally shy-seeming Peterson. Wolfenden's icy clarity of speech was very different from the voice of Peterson, high in pitch, low in volume. Where Wolfenden was worldly, again Peterson seemed the reverse – perhaps to a fault in both cases. Wolfenden had seen the Schools safely into what, did we but know it, would soon be a period of real economic recovery after the war, followed by another period of prolonged expansion. He had sensibly put boarding fees up by some 40 per cent from £180 – little more than three times their level of a century earlier – to about £250 per annum. After their brief fall between 1945 and 1948, numbers had recovered to their earlier level – just below 500. What would Peterson, bolstered by a wave of goodwill, make of his headmastership?

John Magnus Peterson, headmaster 1950–1963, from the portrait by Edward Halliday. Old Salopian, classical scholar and sportsman, he oversaw the Schools' fourth centenary celebrations. His appointments paved the way for a new order.

Physically, the Site was to be little changed, with the modest exceptions of the Queen's Terrace behind the School Buildings, three new houses for masters at Port Hill, and the welcome appearance of a new running-track (the latter greatly assisted by a generous Old Salopian) with its own pavilion on the old Craig Fields. Money, as usual, was tight; but the Fourth Centenary Appeal, which ultimately raised the very useful sum of some £200,000, assisted in these projects, and in a number of House extensions and renovations. The renting of a farmhouse at Talargerwyn helped to liberate some boys from confinement to the Site.

The fourth centenary itself was this time held in the correct year – 1952 – and was appropriately celebrated, starting with a chapel service on 10 February, the actual date of the granting of the original Charter, with the

As part of the celebrations to mark the fourth centenary of the Schools, a new High Cross was presented to the Mayor and Corporation. The arms of the borough and those of the school are engraved on it with a Latin inscription.

Her Majesty Queen Elizabeth II opens the Queen's Terrace in 1952.

Charter itself on the altar. Public celebrations followed in June, with the performance of Paul Dehn's superlative masque *Call-Over* as the outstanding feature, and the year was rounded off in the best possible fashion by the Queen's visit on 24 October to open the new terrace (behind the School Buildings) named after her.

We can see in retrospect that Peterson's headmastership encompassed the final days of the public school as that term used to be understood. A Minister of Education confessed in 1961: 'The fact is, I do not know what a public school is. No one has been able to provide me with a satisfactory definition.' It is not a definition, but a description of the generic attributes, that is the more useful (one might think of high fees, Common Entrance, emphasis on Latin, boarding Houses (usually), intense House spirit, merging into equally intense school spirit at certain moments, a spirit of independence, but an acceptance of both being under authority at the start of one's career and of generally wielding it with fairness towards the close, the rule of boys by boys, a range of traditions jealously maintained, an idiosyncratic vocabulary, daily compulsory games, admiration for athleticism (reflected in 'Colours'), but acceptance of academic ability, the acceptance of compulsory chapel as a central part of school life, probably some corporal punishment, but certainly a range of punishments: everyone will have his own list, but most people 'know' what a public school is in the same way that they 'know' what a cow is, without needing a definition). By the time Peterson retired books were appearing with titles such as *The Public Schools and the Future* and (*post hoc*) *The Public School Revolution* by well-known Headmasters, and the world was irretrievably changing. It is time to return to 1952 and the years that followed.

Twenty-five years after Peterson's retirement from the headmastership, and ten years after his death, it may be possible to view his reign with some sense of perspective, even if consensus cannot be achieved. Peterson the man was widely admired, even loved: this, if anyone, was a good man, a man 'whom you would be ashamed to let down', a man of simplicity, straightforwardness, humility, and compassion, a man who keenly appreciated the best things of nature, literature, the arts, and music. When these attributes are allied to others – his prowess as a scholar, his remarkable ability at a variety of games, and (far from irrelevantly) the fact that he was an Old Salopian – indeed 'one of the best known among all Old Salopians of the present century' – the resulting combination is powerful indeed. Peterson himself, in an important speech to parents in 1963, as he was about to leave the Schools, made known some of his own views about education, and, indeed, in an almost Platonic sense, his views on the good life:

PT display for the Queen's 1952 visit.

> At the risk of appearing quite out of date I think it is just possible to imagine that some of you may have sent your boys to us to experience the disciplined life and be educated in a much wider and deeper sense. If this be so, I wish to make two observations. First, can we agree to explode the extraordinary theory that is quite honestly held by many people today, and practised, subconsciously, by many more – the theory that it is wrong and even dangerous to try to influence or restrain the young in any way? How it can be assumed that the young if left to their own devices will automatically choose what is good and do what is right quite baffles my comprehension. Surely the whole history of mankind and our own experience refute this. However that may be, let it be known that, if you send your boys to us, we shall attempt to influence them in every possible way – and to restrain them too when necessary.
>
> My second point is this. It is fair enough that holidays should be holidays and that not all the rigours of school life should be repeated at home, but on matters of principle I would plead for some consistency of policy. Those of you who allow your sons to smoke and drink at an early age should realise that you are not only making things unnecessarily difficult for the school, but also encouraging in your offspring a way of life that will certainly be expensive, and may lead to an early and tragic end. Furthermore, in the prospectus we boldly claim to instruct our charges in religion and sound learning, and you are all aware that we have a compulsory chapel service every day. Now in all this I make no apology for saying that a true sense of values is not easily acquired if the practice of the home differs fundamentally from what obtains here. Where such conflict exists on matters of principle it is easy to see how the young may suffer from a bewilderment that can soon lead to a sense of frustration, and ultimately to that indignation which exhibits itself in the Angry Young Man of our times. I do not find him an attractive character: the mixture of arrogance and egoism is unpleasing in anybody, and particularly unattractive in the young.
>
> The main point that I want to make, however, is this: there is too much emphasis nowadays on mere academic qualities. In a world in which man has the means to exterminate himself we do not want clever devils; if the accent is to be as much on the noun as on the verb. We are told that there is a great need for more scientists: in my opinion there is an even greater moral vacuum to be filled. . . .
>
> These are not aims that can be preached every day from the house-tops: indeed only my imminent departure makes me break silence now. Virtue is not something that can be taught or learnt in the ordinary way in the classroom: it must be acquired slowly and often painfully. It is a case of 'here a little, there a little, precept upon precept and line upon line'. And, of course, an example must be set too. This is the frightening thing about schoolmastering: the young cannot all see their way through a quadratic equation or a Latin unseen, but they can all see through a sham. Ultimately it is not a question of what a man says, nor indeed of what he does: it is a question of what he is. This surely, and nothing less than this, is the aim of education in the true sense.
>
> This preoccupation with the individual boy and the good life is what makes schoolmastering exacting always, frustrating frequently and occasionally, very occasionally infinitely rewarding.

By his own example Peterson set high standards, still remembered, for others to try to live up to. Such a man will rightly inspire great loyalty.

Was, perhaps, too much expected? As an obituarist acutely observed, 'he was not a man to dominate the school with his presence. Except for a few senior boys, he was a remote figure, dignified but not at ease in the centre of the stage, shunning ostentation, too reserved to seek our conversation and to break down the isolation of his position. When he spoke in public his voice could detract from his sensitive delivery of a fine speech or sermon.'

One result of this and, perhaps, of his personal sorrow, was that Peterson was never a public figure in the way that Wolfenden undoubtedly was. He was a very private person. And here, inevitably, lay a difficulty, because part of a Headmaster's role is essentially public, dealing not only with boys and masters (and Head Boys and Housemasters) but also Old Salopians, the Town (with a capital T), the Headmasters' Conference, parents, and a multiplicity of others. At the same time, the school has to be seen to be progressing, both materially and educationally. In the physical sense, we have seen that the Site altered relatively little under Peterson. Kingsland Grove, not far from Kingsland House, had been bought in 1958, but no new buildings of significance to the boys had been erected since the New Darwin Buildings in 1938 – which meant a period of no less than a quarter of a century by the time of his departure. The school was (it has been argued by an external and reasonably impartial commentator) rather slow to change long-established ways of doing things – and, admittedly soon after his arrival, Peterson even censored a letter to *The Salopian* suggesting, in 1950, that five years after VE-day it was time for enrolment in the CCF to become voluntary rather than, as it still was, well-nigh compulsory.

It would be rash to claim that, even now, any general agreement about Peterson's tenure of office has been reached. As the 1950s drew to their close, and an era of rapidly changing fashions ('pop' music, satire, dress, the Beatles) came nearer, did the Housemasters, senior and generally conservative men, receive from the Headmaster the leadership, decision, discipline, and support which they assuredly wanted and needed? Yet, at the same time, might not the younger masters – some of whom would before long become Housemasters or even Headmasters themselves, and notably good ones, but were not yet working at the 'sharp end' in the way that the Housemasters were – have argued that it was not the Headmaster but the Housemasters who (if anybody) were at fault, through their conservatism and limited visions, while they themselves were being encouraged to explore possibilities of change? That there was a division between the Housemasters and many of the younger staff seems certain. Was the Headmaster a 'liberal' or a 'reactionary'? Here again the opinion is likely to differ according to the viewpoint and age of the Salopian observer of the time, and it is possible, as usual, to see good arguments on both sides. It was a school which happily contained within the system the future founders of *Private Eye*, yet where 'douling', compulsory corps, and compulsory chapel still were the rule, and a school where a tentative advance towards lessening the domination of the classics was achieved, but accompanied by reluctance, for example, to allow a House dance or more casual dress outside school hours, or even the expression of 'challenging' views in the pages of *The Salopian*.

Watching a cricket match from 'The Pier', 1952. The boys in caps are presumably from a local preparatory school.

Certain it seems that, of the masters who had so warmly welcomed Peterson's return in 1950, a number were voicing feelings of disappointment seven or eight years later. Equally certain it is that disquieting intelligence concerning the school's problems reached the ears of at least some Old Salopians. When the dissatisfaction of some of the Housemasters reached its peak as the decade drew to its close, it was inevitable that the Governors, and their devoted Old Salopian Chairman, Duncan Norman, should become involved. Correspondence now in the Library shows how difficult the position had become; and if the interests of the Headmaster and those of some other senior masters are seen to be markedly at variance, how should the matter be resolved? Nobody can envy the Chairman's position. In the end, however, the Governors supported the Headmaster, there were changes and departures among the Housemasters, and the Chairman of Governors himself gave way, before long, to another loyal Old Salopian in Sir Fred Pritchard. To quote again from one of Peterson's obituarists: 'I have always championed his headmastership, but it is not his successes or failures as Headmaster that I remember. Suffice it to say that the spirit and the achievements of the school during his reign – and especially the spirit – do not suffer by comparison with what went before and came after.' That is well and courteously phrased.

It is Peterson the man who will be long remembered, for what he was, not what he did. However, the Governors' decision to succeed him by a man of a very different temperament was as natural as it was inevitable. Yet the roots of many of the changes which were to come over the next decade are almost certainly to be found in the more quiescent period which had preceded it.

WRIGHT

When Donald Wright arrived from Marlborough as Headmaster in 1963, he was just forty. The contrast with his predecessor was marked, for Wright's image is a vivid one. A tall man, a visible man, a man 'always to be seen driving round the Site at 90 mph', a man who might appear at midnight in the Moser Building with a tape-measure, a man whose instinct was to 'turn everything upside down, rattle it, and see if it could be made to work better', not a patient man, a mover and shaker rather than an academic, a man whose new study off the Alington Hall – a hexagon inevitably called 'The Pentagon' – enabled him to see just about everything that could be seen – and be seen by anyone who wanted to look – a man who, however unfairly, gained with a few the reputation of acting first and asking afterwards, a man who, however inadvertently, could allow Butler's statue to be used for hard core, yet a man who simultaneously was famous for his staff work and willingness to consult, and a man so well known that there were occasions when Shrewsbury was referred to as 'Wright's School' – here was the man for the hour. Such men are not, cannot be, popular with all: nor was Churchill in the Second World War. Both saw what had to be done, found the means – human and financial – and did it.

It is essential to view Wright's aims and achievements as an integrated whole for their magnitude to be grasped. A major development plan, conceived and executed with the help of the architect Michael Greenwood, showed the pressing need for new buildings to house the rationalised and modernised curriculum. More classrooms were needed, science and mathematics had to assume a far more important role, a new logic had to be imposed. Buildings need money: hence the central importance of the creation of the Friends of Shrewsbury School and the 1966 Appeal. The change from 'Sides' to 'Sets' called for organization on a wholly new scale: hence the appointments of a Second Master with a real job to do and a Senior Master. A school that was inward-looking, perhaps bored, perhaps almost lost in a 'time-warp', certainly with problems in some areas, needed a new vision: hence younger Housemasters, a new freedom in dress, new freedom to talk with masters, or to get off the Site, to arrange a dance or to go to Stratford, much less emphasis on compulsion, privilege and hierarchy, above all constant discussion and open channels of communication: in short, an Open Society. Again, public schools were under political threat: hence Foundation Awards and some links with local maintained schools.

They say that towards the end of his twelve-year reign Wright felt that he had done all he could for Shrewsbury: if so, it was hardly surprising (though he had found the time to be an influential Chairman of the HMC in 1971); yet he was little more than fifty when he left to become Appointments Advisor to the Archbishops of Canterbury and York and to indulge his enjoyment of music by editing Neville Cardus's writings on that subject. For Shrewsbury, they were twelve wholly remarkable years, the years when 'Sides' gave way to 'Sets', when the arts, drama, music were encouraged to flourish, when the green baize door mentality was successfully challenged in a way that allowed dialogue and friendship to flourish in the vertical as well as the horizontal plane. We have seen that Shrewsbury was largely unaffected by the War. A mercy at the time, it had its drawbacks, in allowing the school long to retain, without too much thought, a range of rules and traditions that had become outdated. Buildings, let it be emphasized, are only one part of Wright's monument, for the transformation which he brought about in virtually every other aspect of the school's life was at least as important and no less enduring. As for the famous 'Pink Book', with its fourteen printed pages of Rules and Privileges, it had become waste paper. We must now look more closely at what happened in these twelve momentous years.

Donald Wright, headmaster 1963–1975, whose achievements as headmaster rival those of his great Victorian predecessors. From the portrait by R. Tollast.

We have already noted that there had been no new individual building of significance erected on the Site since 1938 – a quarter of a century before, before the Second World War – though a number of Houses had added useful and much-needed extensions, and a generous OS benefactor had provided the first proper running-track in 1956. Under Wright, there were major additions to the Site almost from the first: the Lyle Building, significantly, near the Moser Buildings (for the historians and geographers) in 1966, the purchase of 9 Canonbury – later sold – in 1967 as the Headmaster's house, the construction of Kingsland Hall as the Schools' central place to eat, replacing the dining-rooms of the individual Houses, in 1969, the Crafts Centre of 1970, Tudor Court as a senior boys' 'club' in 1972, the major new Science Building (1974), and the almost equally major extension of School House (1974–6) were among the most visible achievements. The School Buildings were extensively altered. There were alterations or additions to the chapel, and the Moser Building (1967) – badly needed, this – while the old Darwin Buildings would be converted into an Arts Centre in 1976, and the fives courts, too, were modernised. This was work on the grand scale; when the 1982 Appeal was launched, the school could announce that almost £1 million had been spent on major projects since 1965 'financed almost equally from school resources and from appeals': Kingsland Hall, the new science laboratories, and the School House extension accounted between them for two-thirds of this large sum.

Kingsland Hall, costing not far short of £250,000, was central and crucial from many points of view. The Governors had long realized the existence, and growing insistence, of domestic problems and difficulties. Of these by far the most worrying and intractable had been to do with House feeding. Most Housemasters were married men with young families. The extent, even limits, to which their wives had to go, in order to ensure that the boys in the Houses had been fed, had become unreasonable and unfair. So much so that with the difficulties of finding cooks and other assistance, and with the strain on Housemasters and their wives growing each term, it seemed only a matter of time before assistant masters thought housemastering not worth the price, or before Housemasters gave up early in their terms of office. That would have been disastrous.

That, therefore, was the primary concern which lay behind the Governing Body's decision to centralise the school's feeding arrangements. But there was a very strong secondary consideration: by going over to central feeding, the schools' dependence on domestic labour in the Houses was drastically reduced. Since there were, at the time, real financial and fiscal concerns to add impetus to the move, such a reduction made sense in every way. Accordingly, in the summer of 1967 the Governors instructed Michael Greenwood (architect of the new Lyle Building, the Moser Building's extension, and the remodelled School Building) to draw up plans for school kitchens and a dining-hall big enough for the whole school at Kingsland House. Work on the site began in May 1968, with the completion date set for mid-July 1969. On 5 November the Hall, which had already been officially opened, was royally 'baptized' by the Queen Mother.

Once it had been accepted that in order to achieve maximum flexibility and economy central feeding had to be in one place and not divided between two, the development of Kingsland House offered a number of practical advantages. In the House itself, the school possessed a large amount of accommodation which at relatively little expense could be adapted internally to provide a dining-room for teaching staff (when they were not lunching with the boys in the central hall), two reception rooms, and self-contained flats, later to be occupied by masters.

There were other consequences, most of them good. Space was saved in the Houses, giving the opportunity to provide more privacy for older boys. In Kingsland Hall, boys were able to mix more. Staff and boys could and did see more of one another. Costs would be kept down. And the school would have a splendid hall which would be available for many occasions, including Old Salopian ones, besides daily meals. Against this, the intimacy of house feeding would inevitably be lost, and the 'family life' of the Houses would have to be remade round other occasions and activities: not impossible aims. So things were seen at the time; twenty years on, Kingsland Hall is recognized as being both necessary and a triumph. The vision of the Governors and Headmaster – and the faith of the Schools' bankers – has been totally vindicated.

At about the same time, another change was taking place, of a very different kind. During 1967, it was decided that the Corps (OTC, JTC, CCF) should henceforth be run on a voluntary basis. Since the end of National Service it had been increasingly hard to find suitable officers, the relevance and logic of some of the training had not been obvious to all, and in general terms faith in a compulsory Corps as one of the cornerstones of the Shrewsbury set-up had waned.

Following a year of broadly based acclimatization, in their second year boys now undergo a programme of camp-craft, map-reading, adventure training and similar activities, i.e. all the non-military side of the Corps. This 'basic year' is regarded as tough – and important. Then, after two years in the school, boys have a choice of joining the Corps (Army or RAF Sections), or a scheme called Senior Projects: they have an obligation to be in one or other of these till they have been in the school for at least four years. (The Corps in 1968 numbered just under thirty strong, compared with perhaps sixty in 1988.) It is interesting that, at the time, a commentator referred to the change as not being 'totally disconnected with the increased permissiveness of our society, both inside and outside Shrewsbury'. It was just seventeen years after the letter to *The Salopian* suggesting a voluntary Corps (to which reference has been made above) had been censored.

Already the range of available activities was becoming wider, not least for those in their first year (ranging from carpentry to chess, painting to printing, decorating to ornithology). Before very long the Sixth Form would have their own 'club' building (with at least some alcoholic liquor available, and occasional 'disco' dances being laid on) in Tudor Court near the tennis courts; the artificial '1970 Club' title with which it was burdened did not long survive.

Almost as important as Kingsland Hall, and nearly as costly, was the New Science Building of 1974. Much thought went into this building, the need for which had become imperative. As the then Head of Science, Peter Hughes, said at the time:

> The advantages we shall gain from the new building are many. When representatives of the Industrial Fund came to look at our laboratories in 1956, they came to the conclusion that our facilities at that time were just about adequate, and so we failed to obtain a grant. During the last 18 years science has expanded enormously: it is now compulsory for all boys in their first two or three years in the school; the sixth form numbers have nearly doubled; and the number of masters has increased from 9 to 14. We have absorbed this increase by modifying the existing buildings, but further modification is impossible. We have only six full-sized laboratories, and all too often boys, masters, and laboratory staff are frustrated because we have to lecture, when a class practical session would be more appropriate. We are well equipped for apparatus, but our storage and preparation facilities are cramped and unsuitable; masters, let alone boys, cannot see what is available.

Three main principles were agreed upon at the outset: first, as nobody could predict with confidence how school science teaching would change in the next decade or so, it was essential that the building should be able to be easily adapted if, for example, there was a move towards more project work, or back to greater emphasis on the lecture/demonstration. This implied flexibility. Second, it was obvious that no one could tell what groupings of the three traditional science subjects would emerge in the future, though the indications from the new Universities suggested that the borderline areas might become more important. This implied that all the science teaching should be housed in one building, preferably of single storey on one level so that all apparatus could be easily transported by trolley from one part to another. Third, it would be highly desirable if the obvious links, of science with mathematics, and increasingly with geography, could be reflected in the physical siting of the building. It would be a mistake to put the building away from the rest of the teaching in the school so that there would be little opportunity for informal contacts in school time; it would be particularly unfortunate if the building was so far away that it became impossible for masters to go over to the common-room for coffee in the break.

With the arrival of this building it was possible (argued Hughes) to look forward to having a science complex second to none among those at the public schools, something which previously had been very far from being the case.

In a way unexpected at the time it can be argued that Wright's task was even heavier in the non-material sphere than in the material and financial one. For this was a difficult time for the public schools (as it soon would be for the Universities). Commenting when Donald Wright left the Schools in 1975, the editor of the *Newsletter* mused:

> More subtle, and less easy to analyse, has been the gradual change in the school to meet the challenges of the fast-moving and bewildering world of the 1960s, a decade of stress and strain if ever there was one. Difficult decisions have had to be taken affecting almost all areas of school life, adapting the body politic to a new age, and at the time retaining the good things of our inheritance. Many schools of our type have found this a traumatic experience, nor have there been obvious answers to all the problems posed, but the fact that Shrewsbury has come through this time, with whatever shortcomings, as a happy and constructive community, is a great tribute to the leadership.

He added that it had been a period 'of remarkable expansion; a period marked by the broad vision of what a school should be in the contemporary world; and a period of strong and positive leadership from the top', all comparable to the period of Alington's headmastership from 1908 to 1916. Numbers in the school had increased by some 20 per cent to over 630. No fewer than two-thirds of the teaching staff, by 1975, were Wright appointments. But that is not all, for it was also the period when public schools ceased to bear any resemblance to the public school of Arnold or Kennedy, to the public school of a thousand bad novels, to the public school of the lurid imagination of its detractors (monastic, therefore homosexual, addicted to corporal punishment, bullying and fagging, games-mad, cribb'd and cabin'd by compulsory chapel and compulsory Corps parades, confined by 'bounds' and 'gating', snobbish and overprivileged yet underfed, worshipping a hundred shibboleths and traditions both archaic and meaningless in 'colours', dress, privileges, and vocabulary). Whether this passing was a 'good' or 'bad' thing is not the subject of this book; opinions are likely to vary, and vary strongly, with the age of the reader. The *laudator temporis acti* is unlikely to see eye to eye with his successor Salopian of the 1980s, though the latter might well feel something in common with his well-known predecessors of the 1950s who went on to found *Private Eye*. May that journal's 'St Cake's' have had its genesis in recollections of Shrewsbury's *Fasti*? Be that as it may, it fell to Wright to be the arbiter, instigator, controller of great, radical, and irreversible change.

Douling was the first to go – by agreement among the boys themselves – by 1965; the Corps, as we have seen, became voluntary in 1967; even more fundamentally, attending a chapel service was no longer compulsory on the former daily basis for all by the early 1970s, and the use of corporal punishment (residual, as we have seen, as early as the 1950s) withered and died. It was far easier to go 'down town'. Yet such changes brought with them, not really paradoxically, other results – noticeably, a loosening of the very powerful loyalty to the school created when it was a tauter, more hierarchical, more self-contained unit. Extended half-terms (understandably welcome to overworked masters) had the same effect, as did broadening contacts in many areas within the world outside (at one time virtually limited to those with a special interest in the Shrewsbury Mission at Liverpool, itself radically changed in 1973 into a Community Centre, with responsibility shared by the school, the Diocese, and the Local Authority). Weekend parties of ten to fifteen people at Talargerwyn, a lofty farmhouse some seven miles from the

Boys at Talargerwyn, Snowdonia, in 1971.

summit of Snowdon, now provide another loosening of school bonds. It is easy to chronicle the facts of these major events, less easy to go behind the facts to the mood of the school as they occurred and the manifestations of discontent.

For while all this was going on under Wright's energetic leadership, it would be absurd to pretend that Shrewsbury somehow managed to miss the traumas of the late 1960s and early 1970s, universal among public schools, much worse in the Universities, and worse still elsewhere, notably in France. Problems with non-co-operation in chapel; outré clothing; long hair; with smoking, drinking, graffiti, and even, on occasion, drugs, were intermittently severe; and via a series of graduated steps – after the retirement in 1966 of Guy Furnivall, chaplain for twenty-five years – the fact of daily compulsory chapel for all came to an end. Indeed, with rising school numbers, this was inevitable, and Houses nowadays have to operate a rota system for attending even those fewer services which are still compulsory. In retrospect, it may be felt that the problems, though not limited to School House, were at their most severe there; plans for a complete structural division of it into two Houses were eventually shelved in the 1970s (being replaced by a much modified scheme), really for financial reasons at a time of rocketing inflation. But it was to prove a difficult time, with Portakabins being used as studies, constant disruption through building works, and a system, for a time, of having two Housemasters although there were not yet two recognizably and physically separate Houses – nor, in the end, were there ever to be. Well intentioned, and even logical, though the experiment was, Eric Anderson determined soon after his arrival that the system was simply not workable, and the House reverted to one Housemaster with a House Tutor, later increased to two. Not before time, for the House had acquired an unenviable reputation for indiscipline and general mayhem (not that it was alone in this).

If the problems at Shrewsbury were no less than elsewhere, they were at least no greater; and it may be argued that Shrewsbury had two important weapons in its armoury not universally available: relative remoteness from major metropolitan areas, and two strong (which does not mean illiberal) Headmasters in Wright and Anderson. Of course, there was ready access to all the products of supermarkets, and nothing could eliminate either that fact or the existence of local pubs. But the period of transition had disagreeable moments, which must have imposed great strains on many numbers of the staff, especially Housemasters, just as they also led to the dismissal of a few members of the school.

Important as new buildings are to meet new or growing needs, other aspects of a school's governance must not be ignored. At Shrewsbury, the position of Senior Master had been attained simply by durability, that is, by the longest-serving master on the staff. There was dignity, but no authority. Wright ensured that the Senior Master would be a deliberate appointment, and that he would have responsibility (broadly speaking) for disciplinary and pastoral matters; at the same time the Second Master – a wholly new appointment – would assume responsibility for academic and certain administrative affairs: it

Opposite: *Early 1920s watercolour by Bernard Gotch, showing the nave and chancel of the school chapel.*

would have been difficult to better his choices of Michael Charlesworth (recently returned from secondment to a headmastership in Pakistan) and Arnold Hagger and, later, Peter Hughes for these important and innovatory positions, which, with some modification, have stood the test of time, though academic matters are now in the hands of a Director of Studies, while the Second (formerly Senior) Master now has a greater responsibility than at first for administration. These appointments must rank in importance with Hardy's appointment of a full-time bursar. At the same time, important curricular changes meant that science subjects would assume their proper importance at O Level; in fact, under Peterson the Classical Fifth had already gone – the form into which scholars and exhibitioners went on entry, taking O Levels at the end of their first year, but in which 'science' was normally limited to mathematics. Such élitism was manifestly becoming not only irrelevant but positively harmful, as was recognized clearly by the able Heads of both Classics and Science at the time. The beneficial effects of the change can be shown in a most striking way. Scholarships to Oxford and Cambridge won in subjects *other than the classics* developed as follows:

1940–9	*1950–9*	*1960–9*	*1970–9*
28	61	66	77

(The disappearance of entrance awards in the 1980s means that the series, unfortunately, cannot be continued.) In effect, the previously accelerated stream was deliberately 'held back', so that a wider range of O Levels is now taken by all at a later stage, in fact the third year in the school, with sciences among the subjects taken by all.

Living arrangements in Houses had long been based upon studies occupied by (perhaps) four to six boys, with 'bedrooms' having typically six to ten occupants: monitors would have the use, in addition, of a 'headroom'. But the arrival of Kingsland Hall changed all that. The disappearance of resident domestic staff (including the 'House John'), together with some alteration of bedrooms and other construction work in Houses, has enabled the creation of study-bedrooms at least for those in their final year, despite the enlargement of the average House's complement from fifty-five to sixty-five. Tentative ideas to match Eton's provision of study-bedrooms for all may have been considered but shelved – at least for the foreseeable future – mainly on the grounds that it is not obviously or necessarily desirable for younger members of the school to be able to achieve the degree of isolation that an individual study-bedroom provides.

EXCURSUS
'HARTFIELD': SHREWSBURY AND THE BLOXHAM PROJECT

The Bloxham Project arose from a conference of Headmasters and chaplains at Bloxham School in 1967. Its aim (which, as it happens, is not especially relevant to this narrative) was to inquire into the way in which Christian ideals were communicated at and by English boarding-schools; the results of the first phase were published in 1973. Shrewsbury was one of the schools involved in the project, though it is disguised as 'Hartfield' in the published accounts,

C GOTCH

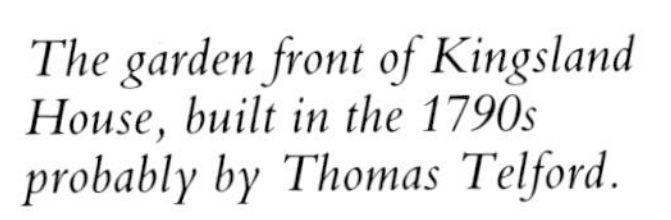

The garden front of Kingsland House, built in the 1790s probably by Thomas Telford.

School House (built as soon as the move to Kingsland took place in 1882) by Sir Arthur Blomfield: Queen Anne revival, 'sweetness and light'.

where, in a pamphlet called *Changes and Chances*, 'Hartfield' received a chapter of its own. This was because, in a long questionnaire, its results were 'markedly different from those of all the other boarding-schools which were visited'. For example, at other schools, the proportion of pupils agreeing with the statement 'there is little trust between pupils and most members of staff' was sometimes as high as 40 per cent: at 'Hartfield', it was only 12 per cent. Were members of staff ready to help with personal problems? At 'Hartfield', one in two said 'yes', whereas elsewhere the proportion was only one in three or one in four. There were many other answers showing satisfaction with discipline, authority, staff–pupil relationships, again in marked contrast with the answers emerging from other schools. Six months later, the sixth-formers involved in the questionnaire were told of the sharply different (from elsewhere) responses which they had given. What was their reaction? The comment of the Salopian who replied lazily 'It's probably because we're all so bloody apathetic' may sound a familiar chord, but it was followed by a discussion in which generally favourable remarks were interspersed with snatches of dissent. The author argues that there is something about 'Hartfield' which both releases the best qualities in its masters and permits those qualities to be seen by the boys:

> He [a master] cares. He is prepared to inconvenience himself for one's own good. He is always available and anxious to help over any problem, no matter how trivial. In teaching he emphasizes to his pupils that it is their own A levels and not his own that are at stake, yet his willingness to help indicates that he genuinely cares. He is prepared to write to the college of a university if it might conceivably help entrance: e.g. I had glandular fever during the summer and first two weeks of this term (my 'Oxbridge' term). He wrote to Cambridge stating this fact (not prompted by me). He is blessed with an excellent temper (I have only once or twice during my whole four years here ever seen him lose it), yet he is very firm, very predictable (one knows exactly where one is with him, so to speak) and is very much respected (as far as I can see) by all who have close contact with him. He is an excellent arguer and it is exceedingly difficult to 'hold one's own' against him. While I was ill with glandular fever, I rang the school up from home asking for books to be sent, and advice on my exam entrance form (Cambridge). He drove up the next day with books and advice, 170 miles in all.

The author of the paper searches deeply for the root causes of 'Hartfield's' success . . .

> That there is no one at Hartfield who is thought of by his colleagues as 'old so-and-so, the diehard reactionary' will sound scarcely believable to many school-teachers. For does not every common-room contain at least one old fogey, who can be depended on to make an authoritarian growl in every coffee-break conversation? The answer would seem to be that if indeed there is no such person at Hartfield then this is by no means an empirical fact similar to 'there are only three men here in their fifties'. Rather, it is a comment on the relationships – on the ebb and flow of sympathy – within the staff as a whole. For if the claim is true, that there are no

The school pavilion and shop, often improved since its original construction in 1882.

diehards at Hartfield, then this must be because no one is pushed into the authoritarian role by the attitudes of his colleagues. It must surely be the case that it is when teachers are most free in the common-room to be themselves, rather than pulled or pushed into roles by their colleagues, that they are also of most use to their pupils. At Hartfield, as compared with certain other schools, there would seem to be relatively few cliques amongst the staff. It has already been mentioned that the masters there claim that there is fairly little confrontation between right wing and left wing on matters of school discipline. Further, there isn't the kind of split between arts specialists and scientists which can occur at some schools (to the point, maybe, where they use entirely separate common-rooms). Nor is there the stereotyping of certain masters as games-players: 'we're littered with Blues,' said one man, 'but there's no clique of games-players, no group of bachelors who all go around together, as at some schools I could mention.' On this whole point of polarisation, it may well be worth mentioning that a small handful of Hartfield

> masters have over the years combined an undisguised radicalism in social and political attitudes with the holding of influential office in the school. This would seem to be a tribute (if tribute is the word) both to the strength of their own characters and also to a certain self-confidence amongst the staff as a whole. One result would appear to have been that younger and less influential masters have not felt pushed into exaggerated postures of criticism; and another that certain boys at least have felt that the school is simultaneously secure and ready to change.
>
> [Again:] If it is so, that there are particular emotional qualities which schoolteachers need to have if their pupils are to trust them, it must follow also that precisely those same qualities need to be demonstrated by head teachers in their dealings with their colleagues. The five qualities which were noted above were: competence, trustworthiness, friendliness, self-knowledge, and the capacity to grant other people freedom in which to move and grow. If it is the case that many boys at Hartfield feel that these are qualities possessed by many of the masters, and if they feel that these are embodied in many of the school's structures, then it must also be the case that these same qualities are perceived by the staff to be possessed by the headmaster.
>
> [Or:] It is relevant to mention that Hartfield has a fairly elaborate personal tutor system for sixth-form boys. This system operates independently of the boarding-houses, and also, to some extent, of the heads of department. But boys are allotted to tutors on the basis of confidential discussions between the Second Master and the Housemaster. The system seems to be working well, though there are some confusions and teething-troubles: 'When are you going to invite me round for a drink?' asked one boy, speaking to his new tutor some time after the beginning of term. The enquiry was needlessly brash, and the master concerned was understandably annoyed. For the fact is that some of the boys have replaced the official phrase 'academic tutor' with their own phrase 'beer man'. ('I was with my beer man last night.' 'I'll have a word about it with my beer man . . .') Several masters are in consequence and at a certain level, extremely irritated. But the important thing to note here is not the abuse of an idea, but the very fact that it is there to be abused. There are clearly several boys, and also quite a large proportion of masters, who take it for granted that beer or sherry should be dispensed when boys visit masters in their homes. ('This didn't happen at all at my previous school,' remarked one man. 'Here it seems the thing to do, so I do it as well.') At the least, this betokens a friendliness at a surface level. The hope (of course) is that it may lead to more personal encounters also.

The author goes on to look at other aspects of 'Hartfield' life – spatial boundaries, emotional boundaries, careers guidance (especially emphasized and successful), 'temporal' boundaries, arts and crafts, games, outdoor activities, the class-room. The author concludes:

> Almost certainly, the main reason for Hartfield's success lies in the fact that it is broadly consistent throughout the many facets of school life. It will have been noted that it is towards the 'progressive' end of the continuum. But so were certain other schools which were visited with the questionnaire, though they were not nearly as contented. Indeed, the school which yielded the highest number of hostile and

> critical responses was one which prides itself on being liberal and progressive. It cannot be concluded that it is a progressive atmosphere as such which leads to contentment: the secret would appear to lie more in consistency and in pattern. The fact remains that it was a broadly progressive school which emerged as the most contented school visited in the study to which this paper relates.

These are but brief extracts from a remarkable document. It is clear that the author was deeply impressed. Of course, he does not assert that all was perfect: 'Hartfield may well have its fair share of problems. They suggest that it's a human and fallible place': there were 'frayed edges' in the community – and quotations from boys are given to display them. Equally clearly, the document as a whole must stand as an enduring monument to the triumph of the revolution at Shrewsbury brought about during and because of the headmastership of Donald Wright. How many Headmasters must have read the 'Hartfield' chapter, have wished that it was their school, and known that it was not.

LOOKING TO THE FUTURE: ANDERSON, LANGDALE, MAIDMENT

Convention, soundly based on good sense and good taste alike, dictates that the historian of a school says little if anything about its most recent years; and who knows whether what seems important now will do so in even ten years' time? It may fairly be said that the relative brevity of the reigns of Eric Anderson and Simon Langdale has been a matter for much more than formal regret: W. E. K. Anderson (born 1936) came to Shrewsbury as Headmaster from Abingdon School in 1975, and, in the fairly distant steps of Alington, went on to become Headmaster of Eton in 1981, ten years after the retirement of Anthony Chenevix-Trench (OS) from that post.

W. E. K. Anderson, headmaster 1975–1980, from the portrait by David Poole. As with his predecessor C. A. Alington, Anderson's successful headship at Shrewsbury led to his appointment as headmaster of Eton.

Eric Anderson had, first of all, the task of consolidating and only then building, both literally and figuratively, upon the achievements of the previous twelve years. Greatly improved use of existing space (e.g. in the School Buildings, Kingsland House, the New House, and, especially, the Old Sanatorium) assisted the advancement of day-boys, about whom a little more will appear shortly, to their rightly enhanced status in the Salopian society – and here he had an exceptional lieutenant in David Gee. If a firm hand could not by itself solve the long-standing problem of the too-large School House, made worse by rapid cost inflation which rendered ambitious building plans impracticable, even if they had been desirable, at least order was restored under a single Housemaster working with an assistant. Grandiose plans for the Arts Centre – the old Chemistry building – were scrapped, and a simpler, but wholly successful design adopted, with William Rushton, one of *Private Eye's* founders, wittily performing the opening ceremony. Squash courts were built in 1979, thanks to a benefaction. Academic standards were consolidated and steadily improved to a very high level of achievement. In five years the Andersons achieved much – more, perhaps, than they realise: what better, more decisive proof than his choice as Headmaster of Eton in 1980? And what better proof of their success at and affection for the Schools than the purchase by the Andersons of a house in Shropshire?

Simon Langdale (born 1937), having been educated at Tonbridge and Cambridge, came to Shrewsbury from Eastbourne College in 1981, leaving his unobtrusively successful incumbency for an appointment outside the world of education in 1988. As these words were being written it was announced that he would be succeeded by F. E. ('Ted') Maidment (born 1942), Headmaster of Ellesmere College. It may be that such shorter incumbencies will increasingly become the rule rather than the exception. Assuredly, the span of 110 years encompassed by Butler, Kennedy, and Moss would not be remotely desirable in the world of today. Important physical developments over the past ten years or so, besides the squash courts (1979), have included the new gymnasium (1983), the conversion of the old gymnasium into a theatre (1984) to hold up to 250 spectators, the conversion of the old Sanatorium into two new Houses for day-boys – Radbrook and Port Hill – and the construction of the first new boarding House (The Grove) since Oldham's Hall in 1911, which was opened in Michaelmas Term 1988. Of these, only the new gymnasium could be said to have made an unflattering impact on the glorious appearance of the Site, situated as it is with somewhat stark and prominent visibility not far from Ingram's and the old gymnasium.

As these words are written, the Schools' numbers, at 651, have rarely been higher, and that without the acceptance of co-education. When fees first moved into four figures around 1974, many Headmasters, bursars, and Governing Bodies must have wondered who would be able to afford them and for how long: yet Shrewsbury's boarding fee for 1989–90 was set at £8,100, and nobody seemed to blench. Facilities are constantly being improved as ever-higher standards are demanded in a competitive world. Public (or, as they are

The Grove is the Schools' most recent boarding House, opened in 1988.

now so often called, independent) schools have adapted in order to survive. No great school can show this more clearly, more spectacularly even, than Shrewsbury with her four foundations. Perhaps Shrewsbury had more to learn from Charles Darwin than to teach him; if so, let nobody doubt that the lesson was both well taught and well learnt.

It is foolhardy to predict the future. But two linked trends deserve notice. The first is that Shrewsbury's catchment area, in common with that of many other schools, is becoming smaller, and less dispersed; the emphasis is on an increasingly local or semi-local constituency, with the north-west of England remaining very well represented, and London and the south-east becoming less so. This, in turn, greatly facilitates half-term exeats and fortnightly weekends at home. At the same time (and here Eric Anderson deserves much credit), the numbers and status of day-boys have been increasing and improving. Time was when, to be candid, boarders, however absurdly and unfairly, were liable to look down on and speak of them in an unflattering fashion; who nowadays even remembers the term Skyte (= Scythian or outcast)? Uncomfortably housed in the School Buildings, formerly in charge of a master rather than a Housemaster, theirs was not an enviable lot. Nor can First Lesson have been welcome. Under Anderson this changed; numbers were encouraged to rise; and, at a time when the public school system seemed to be more under threat than it does today, it made real sense to nourish and strengthen local connections with the professional and mercantile community by ensuring that a significant percentage of the boys in the School had their home in or near Shrewsbury. Today, about one-fifth of the School are day-boys, and, since 1979, they have been divided into two Houses, Radbrook and Port Hill, located in their own buildings at the 'old' Sanatorium. Heads of School now regularly come from day-boys, they naturally have their own areas for eating in Kingsland Hall, and they play a much fuller role in all the school's activities than once was, or could possibly be, the case. It is not too much to describe this welcome and important trend as being, in a sense, a return to the Schools' origins; and much is owed to the determination of their successive Housemasters (as of course they are now termed); and with hindsight the 1967 abolition of First Lesson – anathema to the diehard – can be seen to have played a central role.

Shrewsbury is a well-rounded school. The roles of drama, music, art,and a host of societies have grown enormously over the years. Boys have successfully and to public acclaim built a car – the Invashrew of a few years back – and both they and their masters see much more of the world than did the secluded, unmetropolitan Salopians of a few decades ago, so that the soccer team will go on a 'pre-season tour' to the USA or continental Europe, or the rowing eight to Australia. Self-reliance is fostered by the 'Basic Year'. No longer does one subject dominate the curriculum; no longer does the idiosyncratic language of Salopian slang help to seal off the Salopian from his surroundings; no longer do Hall Elections raise hope or fear in youthful breasts. But all tradition is not lost – if nothing else, the survival of the Hunt shows that, and long may it do so – and praepostors retain some of their ancient dignity. I have said that the Schools' Latin motto is untranslatable; one old, and very free version tried 'We deserve not just censures, and pass by unjust' and, if allowance is made for just a hint of overconfidence, perhaps it may be allowed to stand; certainly it would fit well those great men who at the hours of need were found to head the Schools; and it will be surprising if later generations do not feel able to add some twentieth-century names to those of Ashton, Butler, Kennedy, and Moss.

From the roof of the main school building, a view south east towards the Wrekin.

10

EXCURSUSES

SHREWSBURY IN FICTION

THE Schools provide the setting for several novels, only one of them, perhaps, of real distinction, but none quite without interest, and one of very great local interest indeed. Lionel Birch's *Pyramid* (1921), with its references to A. E. Housman (a poet very popular at Shrewsbury, what with the title of his best-known volume, and the melancholy so appealing to the adolescent mind) and a Headmaster 'reputed to know the text of all Aeschylus off by heart' – probably Moss in the author's mind – has vanished into the large limbo of forgotten novels; I doubt if it is now ever asked for from the School Library. Much the same is true of T. H. Girtin's *Not Entirely Serious* (1958), though it is stretching the facts to call it a Salopian novel except incidentally, despite reference to the House Crier who was 'forced to conclude his message in the manner still prescribed by tradition: "God Save the King – and Down with the Radicals" '. The detective novel *Love Lies Bleeding* (1948), by Edmund Crispin, is set at a school called Castrevenford. But Crispin's real name was Bruce Montgomery, and it was under that name that he taught for two years at Shrewsbury towards the end of the Second World War. There can be no doubt whatsoever that Castrevenford is Shrewsbury, and Crispin makes little attempt to disguise the fact, either in geographical or character-depiction terms: in particular, the maverick 'Mr Etherege' is quite clearly Frank McEachran ('Kek'): 'Mr Etherege was one of those leavening eccentrics who are sometimes to be found at a large public school. . . . He had a fancy for the esoteric and remote, and among his more recent obsessions were Yogi, Notker Balbulus, an obscure eighteenth-century poet named Samuel Smitherson, the lost island of Atlantis and the artistic significance of the Blues. . . . He was flagrantly lacking in public spirit. He never attended important matches. He was not interested in the spiritual welfare of his boys. He lacked respect for the school as an institution. In short, he was impenitently an individualist. . . . His divagations from the approved syllabus were the price that had to be paid, and its evils had in any case been minimised by the removal from his time-table of all work for important examinations.' The plot is centred round a manuscript of Shakespeare's lost play, '*Love's Labour's Won*'; murder is involved, but it hardly seems important.

The novel which matters from the point of view of local interest is Desmond Coke's *The Bending of a Twig* (1906, frequently reprinted). The plot is, in one sense, absurd: a boy unhappily called Lycidas Marsh goes to Shrewsbury with his sole knowledge of public school life ludicrously based upon what he has read about it in a shoal of school stories (*Stalky*, *Eric, or Little by Little*, *Tom Brown*, *The Hill*) provided by his anxious mother. Of course, the luckless Marsh is led thereby into innumerable idiocies in his early days. All that does not matter, nor, really, does what remains of the plot (involving a schooldays-long rivalry with a boy named Russell). What comes through is a remarkably accurate evocation of school life as it is lived. Any prospective Salopian reading it would for a long time have learned a lot that was actually useful, about Hall Elections, douling, the 'Tucks', furnishing a study, rowing, Salopian vocabulary, breaking-up, and much besides. The trouble with school life from the point of view of the average school-story author has been that, unadorned, it is not very interesting, with one term following another without incident. Hence the prevalence, in many stories, of externally introduced adventure, normally of a highly implausible kind. *The Bending of a Twig* eschews all that. When Coke writes 'It is part of Shrewsbury's system that a boy's gradual advance in the school-order should bring him corresponding privileges. His weekly pocket-money doubles; he can write lines or "penals" instead of going to detentions; he does his preparation in his study and no longer in Top Schools', we may be confident that he is indeed describing life at the Schools in the early 1900s; indeed, much of what he tells us was true fifty and more years later.

Finally, Samuel Butler's distinguished novel *The Way of All Flesh* (1903) contains, as has been mentioned already, an unflattering portrait (of which he may have later repented) of Dr Kennedy:

Bedroom in Doctor's Hall, 1954, from a drawing by Samuel Butler, grandson of the headmaster and author of Erewhon.

When Dr Skinner was a very young man, hardly more than five-and-twenty, the head-mastership of Roughborough Grammar School had fallen vacant, and he had been unhesitatingly appointed. The result justified the selection. Dr Skinner's pupils distinguished themselves at whichever University they went to. He moulded their minds after the model of his own, and stamped an impression upon them which was indelible in after-life; whatever else a Roughborough man might be, he was sure to make everyone feel that he was a God-fearing earnest Christian and a Liberal, if not a Radical, in politics. Some boys, of course, were incapable of appreciating the beauty and loftiness of Dr Skinner's nature. Some such boys, alas! there will be in every school; upon them Dr Skinner's hand was very properly a heavy one. His hand was against them, and theirs against him during the whole time of the connection between them. They not only disliked him, but throughout their lives disliked all that reminded them of him. Such boys, however, were in a minority, the spirit of the place being decidedly Skinnerian.

It was in respect of his personal appearance that, if he was vulnerable at all, his weak place was to be found. His hair when he was a young man was red, but after he had taken his degree he had a brain fever which caused him to have his head shaved; when he reappeared he did so wearing a wig, and one which was a good deal further off red that his own hair had been. He not only had never discarded his wig, but year by year it had edged itself a little more and a little more off red, till by the time he was forty, there was not a trace of red remaining, and his wig was brown.

We shall take our leave of this brief conspectus of Salopian fiction with this portrait of the great Headmaster, with the reflection that the facts, as recorded elsewhere, are no less singular.

THE LIBRARY

The Library has been much written about. J. B. Oldham's *Shrewsbury School Library Bindings* (1943) is a classic of its kind – and, by the way, scarce and expensive to buy. And since the Schools' Librarian was also the author of the latest *History* (1952), the chapter on the Library's rare books is, quite naturally, lovingly detailed. For although the (old) Library is not the result of careful collection by a series of bibliophiles – rather, as the present Librarian has put it, it is in essence the library of a country grammar school – it has achieved a perhaps unexpected distinction. The claim (not made by a Salopian) that the Library with its 7,000 or so volumes, is 'probably, for its size, one of the most valuable libraries in the world' might be easier to disprove than to prove; at least it managed to survive the mismanagement (and possible depredations?) of the likes of Atcherley in the eighteenth century. And not only of him, for in 1887 a number of staff members wrote to Moss as follows: 'Among the books the School possesses, we understand there are many which are of value on account of their antiquarian interest; these might be profitably sold and the proceeds of their sale would help to form the nucleus of a library useful both to boys and masters. . . . Hoping that you share our views in the matter, we unite in requesting you to lay this proposal before the Governors at their next meeting' Happily, Moss presumably did not share the masters' views, and, indeed, one of the signatories to the letter, T. E. Pickering, was appointed the

The library at the Old Schools. The school library, founded in 1606, was chained until 1736.

Schools' first Librarian in 1889, and served in that office for twenty-one years. But Shrewsbury has never been rich, and in 1907 the Governors 'sent, secretly, Gower's *Confessio Amantis*, printed by Caxton in 1483, the most valuable book in the Library, to be sold at Sotheby's'. By chance, news of this leaked out, and such was the indignation of boys and Old Boys alike that £1,100 was raised to save it – £140 from the boys alone on their own initiative. This sum was handed over to the Governors on condition that the book should be withdrawn from the auction and made inalienable in perpetuity. One hazards that it might be worth £50,000 to £60,000 today.

The Library naturally contains first editions of books by well-known Old Salopians, even including *Liddell and Scott*, and, among many other Salopiensia, a number of Charles Darwin's letters, two unpublished pages of Samuel Butler's *Erewhon*, and the school archives. There is an important collection of books and manuscripts relating to Shropshire, and interesting collections of early scientific and medical books. The most remarkable MS is the miracle play of *c.* 1430, referred to as the *Shrewsbury Fragment*, but the forty medieval Western manuscripts also include a twelfth-century Juvenal and a

A volume in the present library has been rechained and a shelf of biblical commentaries placed with their fore-edges outwards to show their original titles. The bookcases date from 1829.

thirteenth-century *Liber Sapientiae.* The seventy-three incunabula include the finest copy known of Gower's *Confessio Amantis*, already referred to, and the only copy known of Sulpitius' *Opus Grammaticum* of 1504, produced by Wynkyn de Worde, Caxton's chief assistant and successor. There is a first edition of Spenser's *Faerie Queen* (1590); other *editiones principes* of classical authors include Sophocles, Aristophanes, Cicero, Hesiod, and Cornelius Nepos. First editions of English authors include works by Hooker, Bacon (*Novum Organon*), Donne, Beaumont and Fletcher, Newton's *Principia*, Pope, and Johnson's *Dictionary*, published in 1755. There are seven books printed in England of which no other copy is recorded. And a school with Shrewsbury's classical tradition may feel pleased to possess one odd scrap of paper: 'on it is written the Greek alphabet in diminutive writing, measuring 1 1/4 by 1/32 inches (3.125 cm by 0.08 cm), which is certified by a witness as having been written by the great Greek scholar, Richard Porson, when drunk, at Trinity, Cambridge, on 18 January 1805'. Nor should the discreet and effective connoisseurship of J. B. Oldham in the field of bindings go without a mention.

Also housed in the Moser Building, with more protection nowadays than used to be afforded it, is the collection of nearly eighty English water-colours bequeathed by the astringent assistant master E. B. Moser (1875–1911 and 1915–19) to his old school. It is a charming collection, and made more so by no longer being dominated by the rather brightly bound books in shelves beneath which used to occupy the same room; with works by Turner, Copley, Fielding, David Roberts, Albert Godwin, Helen Allingham, De Wint, David Cox, and Arthur Rackham, there is much quietly to enjoy, even if a drawing (unfortunately described by Oldham as 'perhaps the gem of the whole collection') called 'Mouth of a French River' must no longer be ascribed to Bonington. The portraits possessed by the school are of local rather than artistic interest.

SCHOOL BUILDINGS AND THE SITE

It is easier to write with affection than admiration of the present school buildings, of which only two date from before the move of 1882: the School Buildings themselves (originally the Foundling Hospital, completed by 1765, it had successively become a wool factory, a prisoner-of-war camp, and house of industry, i.e. workhouse), a block which is still (as the Chief Inspector of the Local Government Board reported over 100 years ago) of 'considerable magnitude and solidity'; and Kingsland House, bought in 1930, but built in the 1790s for the influential lawyer Joseph Loxdale, very probably by Thomas Telford, better known as a civil engineer. Curiously enough, the architect of the Foundling Hospital, Thomas Pritchard, is also far better known in another context, as designer of the Ironbridge at Coalbrookdale.

Pevsner deals curtly with the chapel (1887 onwards): 'this of course had to be Gothic at its noblest, i.e. Early English. Red and yellow stone, stepped groups of lancet windows, a somewhat underfed turret in the SE corner. . . . Much early glass by Kempe.' Oldham, a devout man, is a little more flattering

Left: *Antechapel screen (1617) brought from the Old Schools to the new site when the chapel was built in 1887.*

Right: *The carved pulpit also dates from the early seventeenth century and came from the Old Schools' chapel.*

(and since he wrote, the north transept has been redesigned in 1967): 'The very fine Jacobean west screen and the pulpit were incorporated in the new chapel. . . . the seats and the south gallery, originally of pitch pine were in due course replaced in oak, the walls were panelled in oak by Kempe, and stained glass was gradually put into most of the windows. . . . Choir stalls of good nineteenth-century work, formerly in Manchester Cathedral, were presented, and gradually, with richer frontals and hangings, and hand-wrought silver altar and other ornaments, the chapel came to take on a warmth and beauty very different from the bare severity with which it had begun.'

The chapel from 'Central'.

Left: *During the 1890s the school undertook the beautification of the chapel. The carved oak panelling is by Charles Kempe.*

Right: *Sir Arthur Blomfield's* reredos *of 1882, as restored in the 1980s.*

It is tempting to observe of the Moser Building that its most remarkable feature (other than the view) is that its foundation-stone was laid, at a distance and by electricity, by King George V on 3 July 1914. A Latin elegiac quatrain composed by A. F. Chance to celebrate the occasion is best omitted, since it includes a word not found before or since in the Latin language. Its architect, W. A. Forsyth, also designed the Chance Pavilion, and Oldham's Hall (1911), generally accounted, at least up to 1988, the most successfully conceived and executed of the boarding Houses. The Alington Hall (1910) is more remarkable for utility than distinction; an octagonal study, originally for the Headmaster, was added in 1968. The great importance of Kingsland Hall (1969) is alluded to elsewhere, but it lies in function rather than æsthetics; nor can either the appearance or the siting of the new gymnasium (1983) arouse enthusiasm.

The Old Schools, of course, were a different matter. Now the Shrewsbury Library, the Shropshire Libraries in 1983 produced a booklet on its history and restoration. The Old Schools have been described many times; it was a matter for nice judgement as to how much, if anything, should be written here about a set of buildings rightly abandoned by the Schools, on account of theirgrowing and manifest unsuitability, over a hundred years ago. Accordingly, any reader who seeks full details must be referred to other authorities; yet so important were the Old Schools, in many ways – especially educationally – that a brief account is desirable.

There were two main phases of building. The first began in 1595 (as recorded in the School accounts and on a carved stone built into the library wall) and provided for a building of Grinshill stone with a cellar or basement, a ground floor, and two floors above. The accounts show that building work

The Old Schools before the attic was removed, from an aquatint by T. Sanders, circa *1810.*

continued until 1605, and that the ground-floor room was fitted out as a school chapel in the years 1608–17. On the first floor was the school library with a gallery and attics above. About this time, also, a tower block was added to contain the stairs leading to the library. In 1815 the attics were removed and the present Gothic windows inserted in order to increase the height of the library.

The second phase of building was completed in 1630, with a new block built at right angles to the chapel and library. This was also of Grinshill stone and of three storeys, and was designed to provide all the teaching accommodation required, together with rooms for the third and fourth masters. (The Headmaster and Second Master were accommodated in separate houses nearby.) There is some difficulty in determining exactly how this new block was used. A legal brief of 1636 stated: 'The school hath three rooms above stairs for teaching and one below. He that is below in the Accidence School can teach but petties. The three rooms above are distinguished one from the other and none of them [i.e. the three Latin masters] teach but in their own school. And if the headmaster be absent he himself always placeth a substitute till his return; the others use not nor will not meddle in the head school.'

The building of a separate library also indicates that the classical curriculum was itself being widened and enriched through the use of a growing number of printed books on a wide variety of subjects.

The foregoing account relies heavily on the excellent and specialised work of Malcolm Seaborne's *The English School: Its Architecture and Organization, 1370–1870* (1971). On the Schools' even earlier times, Seaborne is also interesting:

> The outstanding Elizabethan example of municipal enterprise in school provision was at Shrewsbury, but buildings specially designed for educational purposes were not completed until the seventeenth century. . . . The remarkable fact is that for the first fifty years of its life this large and successful school was accommodated in a number of ordinary houses bought and adapted for school use. The *alieni* were boarded by householders in the town, possibly in return for domestic services to the families who 'tabled' them. There was no attempt at this date to provide boarding Houses as part of the school organization.

To present-day Salopians, the Site, with its more than 100 acres will be simplicity itself: not so to everybody. A map (p. 130) is essential. In the roughest terms, the boarding Houses encircle the Site, with the exception of Ridgemount and Severn Hill, which form a sort of tail. If we pretend that the Site is a clock, with the School Buildings standing at 12 o'clock, then, very loosely, School House (divided into Doctor's and Headroom, for it is twice as large as the other Houses) is at 1 o'clock; Rigg's at 3; Moser's at 4; Churchill's at 5; Ingram's at 5.30; the new boarding House – the Grove – at 7; the two linked new Dayboys houses (Radbrook and Port Hill) at 8; Severn Hill and Ridgemount at 9 and 10; and Oldham's Hall at 11. It has rarely proved wrong for a school to add to its land bank; the Beck (where Oldham's stands) was acquired in 1890, the Craig Fields in 1891, Withers Field in 1912, land to the east of School House in 1920, Ridgemount and Severn Hill in 1921 and 1924 respectively, and the large area round Kingsland House in 1930. A narrow but important strip of land running roughly from in front of Oldham's to Senior had been acquired earlier in 1899. School House was built as soon as the move to Kingsland took place in 1882; Rigg's and Churchill's (the architect was the idiosyncratic William White of Wimpole Street) followed soon after. Moser's physically dates from 1884–6, Ingram's from 1900, and Oldham's from 1911–12. Much earlier buildings – late eighteenth century – were Ridgemount, which, having once been sold, was reacquired in 1921 and Severn Hill (formerly Chance's), which also was repurchased in 1924–5: both buildings of no little distinction. The two day-boys' Houses were converted in 1979 from the Sanatorium, and another boarding House (The Grove) opened in 1988. The only House name surviving from the Old Schools is Rigg's Hall, because the Housemaster in 1882 was the Revd G. T. Hall, and to have called his House Hall's Hall would have been obviously silly, or at least lacking in euphony. Details of other major building works and purchases can be derived from the map (overleaf).

Overleaf: *Shrewsbury School: a map of the site today. An interesting comparison can be made with the aerial photograph opposite page 132 (Plate 11).*

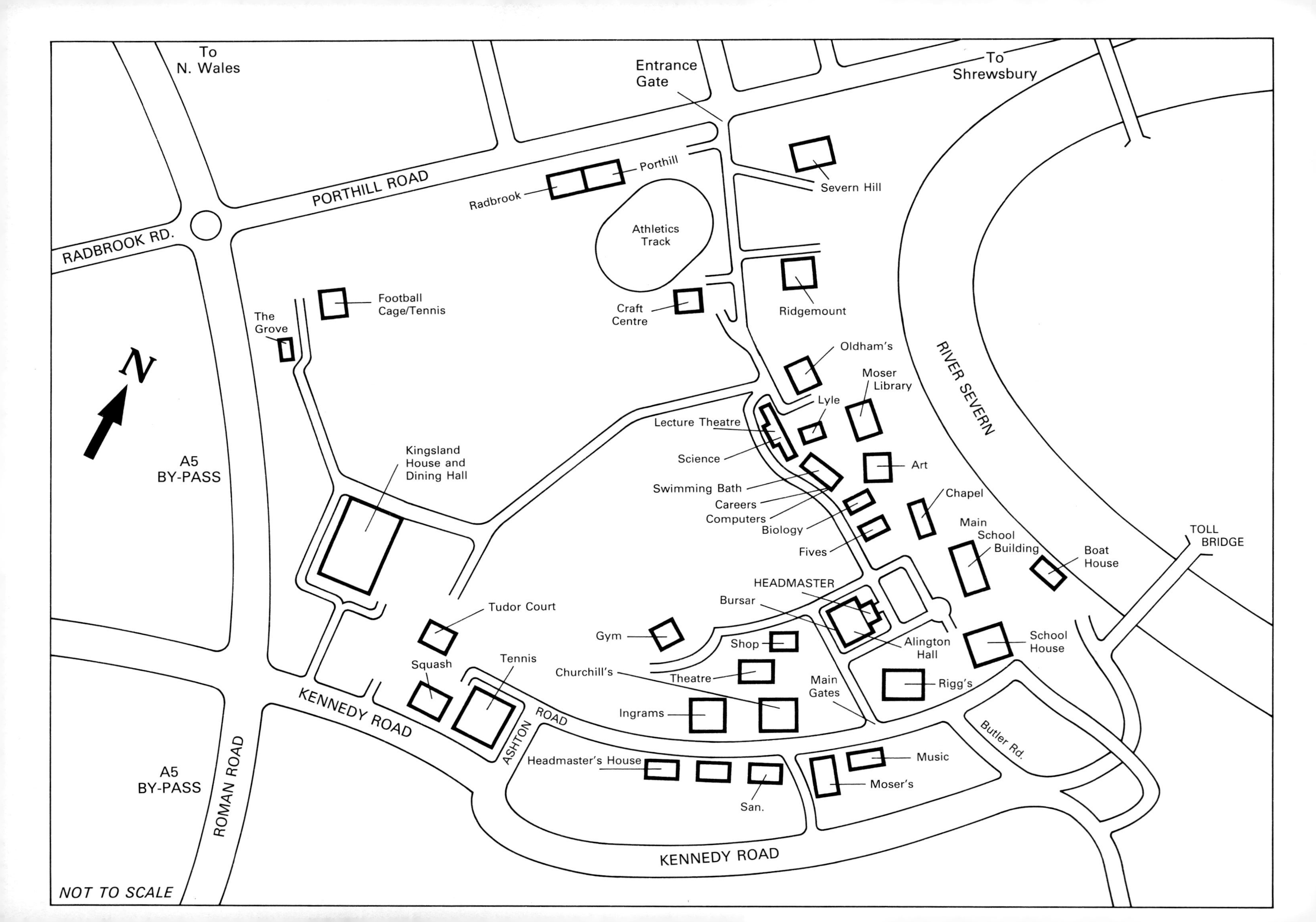
To N. Wales
Entrance Gate
To Shrewsbury
PORTHILL ROAD
RADBROOK RD.
Radbrook
Porthill
Severn Hill
Athletics Track
Craft Centre
Ridgemount
Football Cage/Tennis
The Grove
N
A5 BY-PASS
Kingsland House and Dining Hall
Oldham's
Moser Library
Lyle
Lecture Theatre
Science
Art
RIVER SEVERN
Swimming Bath
Careers
Computers
Biology
Fives
Chapel
Main School Building
Boat House
TOLL BRIDGE
HEADMASTER
Bursar
Alington Hall
School House
Tudor Court
Gym
Shop
Theatre
Churchill's
Squash
Tennis
Main Gates
Rigg's
Ingrams
KENNEDY ROAD
ASHTON ROAD
Headmaster's House
Music
Moser's
San.
Butler Rd.
A5 BY-PASS
ROMAN ROAD
KENNEDY ROAD
NOT TO SCALE

THE MISSION

The history of the School is not that of Shrewsbury House, known at Shrewsbury as the Mission (much of which has been told, with eloquence and affection, by David Bevan in his *Recollections*). Yet the two are strongly linked; and since its foundation in Liverpool in 1903, at a time of dawning social conscience, and the subsequent rationalization and reorganization of its administration on a more efficient basis by H. H. Hardy (who, like Bevan, cared greatly) in 1934, it has meant much to many Salopians and not a little to many inhabitants of the Everton district of Liverpool: inhabitants who are not without their own ways of going about things, perhaps exemplified by the surreptitious removal of the red carpet laid down for the royal opening of the new Community Centre. Beneficial interaction, especially on the games field or in the boxing ring, has been made possible by the successive labours of a series of devoted Missioners, notably James Hill, and starting with Digby Kittermaster. Since the war, and the appalling damage caused by the Blitz, Shrewsbury House has gradually become much more integrated with local parish life. There have been adventures and misadventures, and Liverpool's problems have not grown less or fewer over the years (there is no need to rehearse here the notorious and particular difficulties that have faced the city in the 1970s and 1980s). In 1973 the former Club, or Mission, was replaced,

Scene near Shrewsbury House, the Schools' mission in Liverpool, 1950.

thanks to a scheme evolved jointly by the diocese of Liverpool and the School, by a new Community Centre (officially opened by Princess Anne in 1974), comprising church, boys' club, family facilities, and residential accommodation for social workers. The School now shares responsibility for Shrewsbury House with the local authority and the diocese. Boys from the School – and this surely must be of real benefit – regularly go on three-day working courses to Everton, and, by meeting local boys and their families, learn at first hand just what it is like to live in a modern inner city. It is easy to talk of the 'problems of the inner city', but far more salutary to experience them; and it may be appropriate to add that it was an Old Salopian, Michael Heseltine, who, as Minister of the Environment, was among the first to crusade publicly for help to and the redevelopment of inner cities, and especially Liverpool. For recent times, the changing fortunes of Shrewsbury House have been fully chronicled, for Salopians, in successive issues of the *Newsletter*. Here it must suffice to say that, against all odds, it has survived and more than survived, stony though was the ground in which the seed had to be sown, and its work remains valuably integrated with School activities not only via the courses mentioned above but through regular visits to Shrewsbury by boys and girls from the Community Centre. In one recent year forty-four members and staff went to Shrewsbury on the annual and traditional visit at Whitsun.

Changes (and evolution) have been great. In the 1940s or 1950s (as the Chairman of the Management Committee has pointed out), one Missioner coped from particularly inadequate buildings with the spiritual and material needs of boys only and almost entirely Protestant boys at that. 'Now we endeavour to help the whole community and although closely linked to the Parish Church of St Peter, Everton, we have in the Youth Club a majority of Roman Catholics and, for that matter, a majority of girls.' There is a team in place, with a warden, a youth worker, an assistant youth worker, and a centre manager (but not an Old Salopian among them.) Hostel residents give a hand. As these words are written, a team vicar is still needed. Money, as ever, is short. The 'area has looked like Beirut or Belfast for a while now with all the demolition and waste ground', yet with a new City Council working with local residents in planning the best for the area, there is a rekindled spirit of hope. To see the demolition of high-rise flats in the locality must have been heartening, refurbishment of 'ordinary' houses even more so.

Shrewsbury House would be valuable even if there were no connection with the School; happily the link continues to be strong. The youth worker, asked whether the link between a public school and Shrewsbury House was 'patronising', gave a firm No: 'I believe that these young Evertonians will not be patronised. They see the link between the two as a two-way conduit. Progress in the link is apparent, it does happen, it will continue to happen, provided we keep that conduit open'. And the warden is a co-opted member of the Governing Body.

Of masters at the School, none was ever more closely associated with the Mission than David Bevan, of whom a word. David J. V. Bevan, master from 1929 to 1971, Housemaster of Ridgemount from 1943 to 1954, and Senior

Aerial view of the school in 1986.

Oldham's Hall (1911), generally accounted the most successfully conceived and executed of the boarding Houses (at least up to 1988).

Looking out over Shrewsbury town from the top of the main school building.

Master 1965 to 1971, died aged seventy-nine in 1986. Having represented Oxford at both boxing and swimming, he was appointed 'to a school which he had never seen on the invitation of a headmaster whom he had never met'. He then gave his life to the School, teaching a variety of subjects, but especially history, to School Certificate (later O level) forms, taking over Ridgemount at a desperately difficult time in the war: a war in which he 'underpinned the whole range of school life – social, disciplinary, and organizational'. But he also found time to underpin the Mission, to coach rowing, to run with the Hunt, to play rugger for Shrewsbury Town, even to perform on the stage. He had great personal happiness, and his three sons were in turn head of Oldham's. As was said at his memorial service, 'David Bevan died without any of the honours of this world – but full of honour': indeed so, and he cannot have had an enemy in the world. Let him stand for the many masters who unselfishly gave their lives to Shrewsbury, but whose sole memorial is a notice in the *Newsletter* on their retirement or death. It is difficult to believe that the memory of his name will readily fade at Shrewsbury House.

Carmen Salopiense

1 Rex Edwarde, te canamus
Pium Fundatorem,
Nec, sodales sileamus
Regiam sororem
Mente prosequamur grata
Regem et reginam,
Fautricemque amoena prata
Resonent Sabrinam.
Floreat Salopia!

2 Non tacendumst hic priorum
Nobilem cohortem:
Plenam vitam huic honorum,
Pleniorem mortem:
Illius nec nomen turpis
Obruat robigo,
Qui humanae docet stirpis
Unde sit origo.
Floreat Salopia!

3 Ceteri dum magistrorum
Lugent breve fatum,
Fas iactare Informatorum
Hic triumviratum:
Nostra tum iubente nympha
(Rudis forte si sis)
Exardebat Cami lympha,
Exardebat Isis.
Floreat Salopia!

4 Nimiis stipata turbis
Annis plus trecenis,
Sedem schola liquit urbis
Imparem Camenis:
Nescit studium mutari,
Quique alumnos pridem
Nominis amor praeclari
Nos exercet idem.
Floreat Salopia!

5 Editique caro colle
Matri quam amamus
Arte, libro, remo, folle
Gloriam petamus:
Sic futuros hic per annos
Laus accumuletur,
Sic per ultimos Britannos
Nomen celebretur.
Floreat Salopia!

C. A. Alington

Headmasters of Shrewsbury School

Thomas Ashton	1561–1571
Thomas Lawrence	1571–1583
John Meighen	1583–1635
Thomas Chaloner	1637–1645
Richard Pigott	1646–1662
Thomas Chaloner	1663–1664
Andrew Taylor	1664–1687
Richard Lloyd	1687–1723
Hugh Owen	1723–1727
Robert Phillips	1727–1735
Leonard Hotchkis	1735–1754
Charles Newling	1754–1770
James Atcherley	1771–1798
Samuel Butler	1798–1836
Benjamin Hall Kennedy	1836–1866
Henry Whitehead Moss	1866–1908
Cyril Argentine Alington	1908–1916
Harold Athelstane Parry Sawyer	1917–1932
Henry Harrison Hardy	1932–1944
John Frederick Wolfenden	1944–1950
John Magnus Peterson	1950–1963
Arthur Robert Donald Wright	1963–1975
William Eric Kinloch Anderson	1975–1980
Simon John Bartholomew Langdale	1981–1988
Francis Edward Maidment	1988–

11

SOME OLD SALOPIANS

WHEN J. B. Oldham drew up his list of distinguished Old Salopians in 1952, he limited himself to deceased Old Salopians who had achieved inclusion in the *Dictionary of National Biography*. He listed approximately 140 names. The list that follows retains only about fifty of these, and adds another sixty or so, mostly but not entirely from the modern era. It includes quite a number of those still living, chosen upon necessarily eclectic principles, one of those being likelihood of recognition by non-Salopians. There will assuredly be sins (despite all efforts) of omission, for all of which the author must accept responsibility; after all, there have been some 15,000 Salopians since the year 1800. The list includes one Honorary OS (Neville Cardus), but still excludes that historical figure 'Martin Marprelate' who cannot certainly be identified with the Salopian who bore his real name, John Penry, at about the right time. As 'Martin Marprelate' was hanged in 1593, perhaps we should not be over-keen to make the identification.

What happens to Salopians in later life? A register was prepared by H. N. Dawson in 1958. If one looks at those who entered the Schools in 1927 and 1928 – and were thus in their early forties, or mid-career, when the Register was compiled – the following results can be derived from the 240 boys who entered Shrewsbury in those years. In percentage terms (rounded off), we find that the subsequent careers of 26 per cent are unknown; 22 per cent went into the professions (doctor, architect, solicitor, barrister, etc.); 22 per cent went into business; 12 per cent were dead, mainly killed in action in the Second World War (in which 224 Old Salopians lost their lives); 5 per cent were farmers; 5 per cent in academic life; 3 per cent in the Civil Service; and 5 per cent in a variety of other occupations, including the Church and the Services. Just one of them – an Olympic Gold Medallist – appears in the list of the distinguished Old Salopians that follows; it is perhaps noteworthy that there is not even one MP, never mind a Cabinet Minister among them. There is no reason to suppose that the foregoing is at all untypical, with its emphasis on business and the professions (about two-thirds of those who survived the war and whose subsequent career is known), though the numbers in academic life, the Church, and the Civil Service seem lower than one might expect.

SELECTED LIST OF OLD SALOPIANS

ANDREW DOWNES (1562), ?1549–1628, Greek scholar; Regius Professor of Greek at Cambridge for thirty-nine years; took part in producing the Authorized Version of the Bible; described by contemporaries as 'a walking library'.

SIR PHILIP SIDNEY (1564), 1554–86, soldier, statesman, diplomat, and poet; named after his godfather, Philip II of Spain, against whom he was fighting when mortally wounded at Zutphen. His statue forms the school memorial for the 1914–18 War.

SIR FULKE GREVILLE 1st Lord Brooke (1564), 1554–1628, poet and statesman; intimate friend and biographer of Philip Sidney, both having entered the School the same day; Chancellor of the Exchequer.

SIR RANDOLPH CREW (*c.* 1571), 1559–1646, politician and judge; Speaker of the House of Commons; Chief Justice (King's Bench). A judgement of his has been described as 'perhaps the grandest passage of sonorous prose ever spoken from the English Bench', concluding: 'Where is Bohun? Where's Mowbray? Where's Mortimer? Nay, which is more, and most of all, where is Plantagenet? They are intombed in the urns and sepulchres of mortality. And yet let the name and dignity of de Vere stand so long as it pleaseth God.'

SIR THOMAS CREW (1581), 1565–1634, Speaker of the House of Commons; defended the liberties of Parliament against James I as being 'matters of inheritance, not of grace'.

PIERS GRIFFITH (1584), d. 1628, naval adventurer; said to have fought in the fleet against the Armada, and to have taken part in some of Drake's expeditions against Spain; thought to have been the Welsh pirate named Griffith taken at Cork in 1603; buried in Westminster Abbey.

SIR ARTHUR HOPTON (1597), ?1588–1614, astrologer and mathematician.

SAMPSON PRICE (1601), 1585–1630, divine, preacher, and controversialist; called, on account of his attacks on the papists, 'malleus haereticorum'; chaplain to James I and Charles I.

SIR THOMAS JONES (1623), 1614–92, Chief Justice (Common Pleas); MP for Shrewsbury; during the Civil War trimmed between the two sides; when James II determined to obtain a decision in favour of the dispensing powder in the case of 'Godden *v.* Hales', and told the Chief Justice, 'I am determined to have twelve judges who will be all of my mind as to this matter', Jones's reply was, 'Your Majesty may find twelve Judges of your mind, but hardly twelve lawyers'; dismissed from office in consequence.

RICHARD ALLESTREE (1633), 1619–81, Royalist divine; served as private soldier at Edgehill; later, though ordained, employed on missions between Charles II in exile and his supporters in England; captured and imprisoned; after the Restoration became chaplain to Charles II; Regius Professor of Divinity at Oxford; Provost of Eton College, where he built at his own expense the west side of the outer court.

SIR GEORGE SAVILE 1st Marquis of Halifax (1642), 1633–95; statesman and author; known as 'The Trimmer'; secured the defeat of the Exclusion Bill; opposed repeal of the Test Act; employed by James II to seek a compromise with William of Orange; on behalf of the Lords and Commons offered the crown to William and Mary; wrote brilliant political tracts, including *The Character of a Trimmer* and the *Character of Charles II.*

SIR WILLIAM WILLIAMS (1649), 1634–1700, barrister and Speaker of the House of Commons; strongly supported the anti-court party in Charles II's reign, and appeared in many political lawsuits on the side opposed to the Crown; became the bitter enemy of Jeffreys, another Old Salopian, especially after he had, as Speaker, reprimanded him, kneeling at the Bar, in extravagantly coarse terms; later became Solicitor-General, his abilities and knowledge being 'such that he completely threw his superior into the shade'; appeared for the Crown in the prosecution of the Seven Bishops, having been given to understand that if he obtained a conviction he should replace his old enemy, Jeffreys, as Lord Chancellor; described as being now, 'next to Jeffreys, perhaps the best hated man in England'.

SIR GEORGE JEFFREYS 1st Lord Jeffreys (1652), 1645–89, judge, excelled in civil cases when not politically prejudiced, but notorious for his severity in criminal ones; supported court party and opposed the exclusion of James II; presided at the 'Bloody Assize' after Sedgemoor, and at trials of Baxter and Titus Oates; Chief Justice under Charles II, and appointed Lord Chancellor by James II; imprisoned after James II's flight, and died in the Tower.

SIR THOMAS POWYS (1663), 1649–1719, MP and judge; was appointed Attorney-General, and, as such, led for the Crown in the prosecution of the Seven Bishops.

JOHN WEAVER (*c.* 1683), 1673–1760, dancing master at Shrewsbury, and introducer into England of ballet (then known as 'pantomime'); produced many ballets, usually at Drury Lane.

AMBROSE PHILIPS (*c.* 1685), 1674–1749, poet; started *The Freethinker*, which ran to three volumes; wrote two plays and various works in prose and verse; best known for his *Pastorals*, which excited the ridicule, as well as the jealousy of Pope; his name and literary style were the origin of the word 'namby-pamby'.

WILLIAM ADAMS (*c.* 1715), 1706–89, divine, Master of Pembroke College, Oxford; wrote reply to Hume's 'Essay on Miracles'; lifelong friend of Dr Johnson.

JOHN TAYLOR (*c.* 1715), 1704–66, classical scholar, commonly known as 'Demosthenes' Taylor; Registrary and Librarian of Cambridge University; Fellow of the Royal Society; published editions of Lysias, Demosthenes, and Aeschines.

CHARLES BURNEY (1737), 1726–1814, musician and author, taught music and published his own compositions; Fellow of the Royal Society and foreign member of the Institut de France; after several continental tours to collect material, produced his monumental *History of Music*; intimate friend of Johnson, Garrick, Burke, and Reynolds, and father of Fanny Burney, Madame d'Arblay, who wrote his biography; commemorated by a tablet in Westminster Abbey.

EDWARD WARING (*c.* 1745), 1734–98, mathematician, senior wrangler; appointed before he was strictly qualified, at the age of twenty-five, Lucasian Professor of Mathematics at Cambridge; Fellow of the Royal Society; took MD and practised for a short time as a physician; gained an international reputation by a book described as 'one of the abstruse books written on the abstrusest parts of algebra'.

SIR JOHN FLOYD (*c.* 1758), 1748–1818, general; entered the army at the age of twelve, and at fifteen made riding master to his regiment, Elliott's Light Horse; described as 'the most accomplished English cavalry commander who ever served in the south of India'; fought with distinction under Lord Cornwallis against Tippoo Sultan, and later, as major-general, commanded the covering army at the siege of Seringapatam.

HUGH OWEN (*c.* 1771), 1761–1827, antiquary, Archdeacon of Salop; collaborated with the Revd J. B. Blakeway in the monumental *History of Shrewsbury*.

JOHN BRICKDALE BLAKEWAY (1772), 1765–1826; antiquary; called to the Bar, but subsequently ordained; published sermons and works on the authorship of the *Letters of Junius*, but his fame rests on the *History of Shrewsbury* written jointly with Archdeacon Hugh Owen, and *Sheriffs of Shropshire*.

CHARLES ROBERT DARWIN (1818), 1809–82, naturalist; commemorated at Shrewsbury by a statue in front of the Old Schools.

BENJAMIN HALL KENNEDY (1819), 1804–89, classical scholar and Headmaster of Shrewsbury; Professor of Greek at Cambridge.

WILLIAM FARR (*c.* 1820), 1807–83, statistician; Fellow of the Royal Society; practised as a physician, and through his interest in medicine virtually founded the scientific study of vital statistics.

GEORGE HENRY SACHEVERELL JOHNSON (1821), 1808–81, versatile scholar, won the Ireland; examiner in mathematics at Oxford; Fellow of the Royal Society; Savilian Professor of Astronomy; Whyte Professor of Moral Philosophy; Dean of Wells; wrote on the Psalms.

WILLIAM HENRY BATESON (1825), 1812–81, Master of St John's College, Cambridge; took an important part in University administration; member of the Commission to inquire into the property and income of the two Universities.

RICHARD SHILLETO (1825), 1809–76, classical scholar; through having married early was not eligible for a fellowship, and spent thirty years coaching at Cambridge; doing 'the work that the colleges ought to have done'; in 1867 elected Fellow of Peterhouse.

FREDERICK WILLIAM FABER (1826), 1814–63, hymn-writer and Roman Catholic divine; he came under the influence of the Oxford Movement while an undergraduate; ordained and held a living in the Church of England, but in 1845 joined the Church of Rome.

ROBERT SCOTT (1826), 1811–87, classical scholar and divine; after a distinguished academic career at Christ Church, Oxford, was ordained, elected Master of Balliol in opposition to Jowett; Dean of Rochester; best-known book the Greek-English lexicon compiled in conjunction with Liddell.

GATHORNE HARDY, 1st Earl of Cranbook (1827), 1814–1906, statesman; called to the Bar, but soon took up politics on the Conservative side, supporting in particular the Church of England; elected MP first for Leominster, then, in opposition to Gladstone, for Oxford University; entered the Cabinet in 1866, being successively Home Secretary, Secretary of State for War, and Secretary for India; Lord President of the Council; unexpectedly passed over as successor to Disraeli in leadership of the House of Commons.

SIR ROBERT PHAYRE (1829), 1820–97, soldier, served in the Afghan Wars and in the Mutiny; resident at Baroda, and, as a result of his criticism of the Gaekwar, an attempt was made at the latter's instigation to poison him.

GEORGE AUGUSTUS CHICHESTER MAY (1830), 1815–92, Irish judge; Lord Chief Justice of Ireland.

SIR CHARLES THOMAS NEWTON (1831), 1816–94, archaeologist, held consular posts in the Levant; succeeded in obtaining for the Museum the remains of the Mausoleum of Halicarnassus; largely responsible for the foundation of the Society for the Promotion of Hellenic Studies, the British School at Athens, and the Egyptian Exploration Fund.

SIR CHARLES SLADEN (1831), 1816–84, Australian statesman; emigrated to Victoria; soon entered politics, and became leader of the Conservative party in the Legislative Council; for a short time Prime Minister.

WILLIAM THOMSON (1831), 1819–90, Archbishop of York; while still an undergraduate practically completed *Outlines of the Laws of Thought*, which 'in some respects anticipated Mill's *System of Logic*'; Provost of Queen's College, Oxford; Bishop of Gloucester and Bristol, but within ten months of his consecration translated to York, where he was Archbishop for more than twenty-eight years.

WILLIAM WALSHAM HOW (1832), 1823–79, divine; early gained a reputation for his pastoral work, and refused five colonial bishoprics before accepting the suffragan bishopric of Bedford in London diocese; wrote hymns.

HUGH ANDREW JOHNSTONE MUNRO (1833), 1819–85, classical scholar; Fellow of Trinity College, Cambridge; among his works on the classics his edition of Lucretius was outstanding (1864), 'recognized as the most valuable contribution to Latin scholarship that any Englishman had made during the century'.

JOHN EYTON BICKERSTETH MAYOR (1838), 1825–1910, classical scholar; for a short time master at Marlborough College; Fellow of St John's College, Cambridge; succeeded H. A. J. Munro as Kennedy Professor of Latin; original Fellow of the British Academy; for a short time University Librarian.

HENRY ARTHUR MORGAN (1843), 1830–1912; Master of Jesus College, Cambridge, 1885–1912.

SAMUEL BUTLER (1848), 1835–1902, philosophical writer; made his name as a writer by his characteristically satirical *Erewhon* (originally published anonymously); controverted the views of his fellow-Salopian, Darwin; wrote on topography, art, Homer, and varied other subjects; published the *Life and Letters* of

his grandfather, the Headmaster of Shrewsbury; his autobiography, in the form of a novel, *The Way of all Flesh*, was published posthumously.

SAMUEL MOORE (1852), 1838–1811, friend of Engels; first translator of Karl Marx's *Das Kapital* into English.

WILLIAM EMERTON HEITLAND (1862), 1847–1935, Roman historian, author of *The Roman Republic*.

RICHARD DACRE HODGSON (later Archer-Hind) (1862), 1849–1910, Greek scholar and Platonist; spent most of his time teaching as Fellow of Trinity College, Cambridge.

THOMAS ETHELBERT PAGE (1866), 1850–1936, classical scholar and teacher; for thirty-seven years Sixth Form master at Charterhouse – 'pre-eminent among the assistant masters of his day'; for twenty-five years editor-in-chief of the Loeb Classical Library.

GRAHAM WALLAS (1871), 1858–1932, political thinker; taught first in schools, then as University extension lecturer, and lastly at the London School of Economics.

STANLEY JOHN WEYMAN (1871), 1855–1928, novelist; made his name first by *A Gentleman of France*.

HENRY WOODD NEVINSON (1873), 1856–1941, journalist and war correspondent; a vigorous defender of those whom he considered oppressed; had a genius for finding himself in the most troubled spots, such as the Graeco-Turkish war, Ladysmith during the siege, street fighting in Moscow and Barcelona, Morocco, the Balkans and, in the First War, the Dardanelles.

WILLIAM JOSEPH MYLES STARKIE (1877), 1860–1920, classical scholar; President of Queen's College, Galway.

SIR OWEN SEAMAN (1878), 1861–1936, poet and satirist; for thirty-five years on the staff of *Punch*, and editor for twenty-six.

JOHN LEWIS ALEXANDER PATON (1879), 1863–1946, outstanding High Master of Manchester Grammar School, 1903–23.

SIR RICHARD SOMERS TRAVERS CHRISTMAS HUMPHREYS (1882), 1867–1956, Recorder of Cambridge, 1926; King's Bench judge; Privy Councillor; 'The story of Humphreys' life is the story of the criminal law of his time'; appeared in or presided at trials of Oscar Wilde, Crippen, F. H. Seddon, G. J. Smith ('Brides in the bath'), R. Casement, H. Bottomley, Bywaters and Thompson, Mrs Rattenbury, and J. C. Haigh (the 'acid bath murderer').

SIR WILLIAM BEACH THOMAS (1882), 1868–1957; author, journalist, countryman, and war correspondent.

DESMOND FRANCIS TALBOT COKE (1893), 1879–1913; author of *The Bending of a Twig* (and many other books).

SIR FRANCIS HENRY HUMPHRYS (1893), 1879–1971; Plenipotentiary to Amir of Afghanistan, 1922; High Commissioner in Iraq, 1929, and subsequently Ambassador; played cricket for Oxford in 1900 against the Australians and three times took the wicket of W. G. Grace.

ALAN JOHN BAYARD WACE (1893), 1879–1957; archaeologist and excavator of Mycenae; Director of British School at Athens, 1914–1923.

SIR HENRY PAGE CROFT, 1st Baron Croft (1896), 1881–1947, politician; MP for thirty years as a Conservative, achieving prominence by his unflagging work as an imperialist and supporter of Tariff Reform; Under-Secretary of State for War during Second World War.

EDWARD FRANCIS PAGET (1900), 1886–1971; Archbishop of Central Africa, 1955–7.

MAURICE PLATNAUER (1901), 1887–1974; classical scholar; editor of plays of Euripides and Aristophanes; Principal of Brasenose College, Oxford, 1956–60.

ERIC ARTHUR BARBER (1901), 1888–1965; classical scholar; Rector of Exeter College, Oxford, 1943–56; Editor of Propertius (with H. E. Butler).

SIR BERNARD CHARLES TOLVER PAGET (1901), 1887–1961; General; C.-in-C. Home Forces, Second World War; 'The greatest trainer of British troops for battle since Sir John Moore'.

WILLIAM AUBREY CECIL DARLINGTON (1904), 1890–1979; theatre critic of *Daily Telegraph*; wrote of Dame Edith Evans, as Nurse in *Romeo and Juliet* 'As earthy as a potato, as slow as a carthorse, and as cunning as a badger.'

SIR MILES CHRISTOPHER DEMPSEY (1911), 1897–1960; General; Commander of Second Army, NW Europe, 1944–5; C.-in-C. SE. Asia, 1945; C.-in-C. Middle East, 1946–7; ADC General to King George VI, 1946.

ALLAN ALBERT BLAKEWAY (1912), 1898–1936, classical archaeologist; Director, British School at Athens, 1936.

SIR NEVILLE CARDUS (Hon. OS; staff 1912), 1889–1975; author and journalist on music and cricket; cricket coach at Shrewsbury (1912–16); wrote that 'because [R. D. F. Bland] has played cricket at Shrewsbury School . . . he is one of the blest of the earth'.

NEVIL SHUTE NORWAY (1913), 1899–1960, as Nevil Shute, best-selling novelist (*A Town like Alice* etc.).

SIR FRED EILLS PRITCHARD (1913), 1899–1982, High Court Judge; Chairman of Governing Body of Shrewsbury School, 1960.

RICHARD KIDSTON LAW (Lord Coleraine) (1915), 1901–80, politician, Minister of Education (1945).

ANDREW COMYN IRVINE (1916), 1902–24, mountaineer; died with Mallory on Mt Everest near or at the top.

SIR RICHARD FELIX SUMMERS (1916), 1902–77, Chairman, John Summers & Sons Ltd; President, British Iron and Steel Federation, 1960; High Sheriff of Flint, 1944–5; Member of Governing Body.

ROBERT LESLIE HOWLAND (1919), 1905–86, Fellow and President of St John's, Cambridge; putt shot in Olympic Games, 1928; English native record holder for putting the weight.

SIR EDGAR CUTHBERT FREMANTLE WHITEHEAD (1919), 1905–71, KCMG; Prime Minister of Southern Rhodesia, 1958–62.

SIR BASIL SMALLPEICE (1920), 1906– , industrialist (Managing Director, BOAC; Chairman, Cunard Steam Ship Co. Ltd, 1965–71); autobiography, *Of Comets and Queens*, 1981.

JOHN GERALD HEATH LANDER (1921), ca 1907–1941, oarsman (Gold Medallist, Coxswainless Fours, Olympic Games, 1928).

ROBERT MORTON NEWBURGH TISDALL (1921), 1907– ; Olympic Gold Medallist (400 metres hurdles), 1932; former holder of unofficial world record for the distance.

SIR FRANCIS JOHN BAGOTT WATSON (1921), 1907– , Director, the Wallace Collection, 1963–74; Slade Professor of Fine Art, Oxford, 1969–70; author.

MAX LEONARD ROSENHEIM (Lord) (1922), 1908–72, Professor of Medicine, University of London; Chairman of the Medicine Commission.

JOHN LANGSHAW AUSTIN (1924), 1911–60, White's Professor of Moral Philosophy, Oxford University; author of *Sense and Sensibilia*; President, Aristotelian Society, 1956–7; Junior Proctor, 1949–50.

SIR ARTHUR ERIC COURTNEY DRAKE (1924), 1910– , Chairman, British Petroleum PLC, 1969–75.

GENERAL SIR GEOFFREY RANDOLPH DIXON MUSSON (1924), 1910– , Adjutant-General, 1967–70.

SIR NORMAN JOHN SKELHORN (1925), 1909–88, Director of Public Prosecutions, 1964–77.

FRANCIS EDWARD HOVELL-THURLOW CUMMING-BRUCE (Lord Thurlow) (1925), 1912– , politician and diplomat; Governor and C.-in-C. of Bahamas, 1968–72.

JAMES ROUALEYN HOVELL-THURLOW CUMMING-BRUCE (Hon) (1925), 1912– , Chancellor, Diocese of Ripon; Lord Justice of Appeal, 1977–85.

PAUL EDWARD DEHN (1926), 1912–76; author and poet; wrote the masque *Call Over* for the Quatercentenary celebrations; wrote many film scripts, including *The Spy Who Came In From The Cold.*

SIR GEORGE DONALD ALASTAIR MACDOUGAL (1926), 1912– , author, scholar, economist, administrator, Economic Director, NEDO, 1962–4; Head of Government Economic Service, 1969–73.

JOHN HYRNE TUCKER WILSON (1928), 1914– , oarsman, Olympic Gold Medallist (pairs), 1948.

SIR ARTHUR WILLIAM PETERSON (1929), 1916–86, Permanent Under-Secretary, Home Office, 1972–7.

RICHARD CHARLES COBB (1931), 1917– , Professor of Modern History at Oxford, 1973–84; prolific author and autobiographer.

RICHARD HOPE HILLARY (1931), 1919–43, Battle of Britain fighter pilot; author of *The Last Enemy*.

GEOFFREY DAWSON LANE (Lord) (1931), 1918– , Lord Chief Justice of England.

SIR CHARLES MARTIN LE QUESNE (1931), 1917– , Ambassador to Algeria, 1968–71; High Commissioner in Nigeria 1974–76.

HENRY WILLIAM RAWSON WADE (1931), 1918– , Professor of Law, Oxford University 1961–76; Professor of English Law, Cambridge University, 1978–82.

SIR ROBERT CHARLES EVANS (1932), 1918– , as mountaineer, was member of successful 1953 Mt Everest expedition; Vice-Chancellor, University of Wales, 1965–7 and 1971–3; Principal, University College of N. Wales, 1958–84.

ANTHONY CHENEVIX-TRENCH (1932), 1919–79, Headmaster of Bradfield, Eton, and Fettes.

RICHARD ANDREW PALETHORPE-TODD (1932), 1919– (now Richard Todd), film actor, *The Dam Busters* and many others.

SIR PETER ALLAN RENSHAW BLAKER (1936), 1922– , barrister; HM Foreign Service; Minister of State, FCO, 1979–81.

FRANCIS HENRY KING (1936), 1923– , CBE; novelist and critic; drama critic *Sunday Telegraph* (1976–88); President of

International PEN (1986–9); winner of Somerset Maugham, Katherine Mansfield, and *Yorkshire Post* awards for Literature.

SIR JOHN GODFRAY LE QUESNE (1937), 1924– , sometime Chairman, Monopolies and Mergers Commission.

SIR HENRY FREDERICK ROSS CATHERWOOD (1938), 1925– , Member, European Parliament since 1984; Director-General, NEDC, 1966–71; businessman and economist.

SIR JOHN GRAHAM CUCKNEY (1939), 1925– , leading industrialist and company chairman; as Chairman of Westland, involved in public quarrel with M. R. D. Heseltine (OS), Minister of Defence.

RONALD ERNEST UTIGER (1940), 1926– , Chairman, TI Group, 1984–9; Governor, NIESR from 1983.

JAMES BRIAN EDWARDS HUTTON (1945), 1931– , Lord Chief Justice, Northern Ireland.

MICHAEL RAY DIBDIN HESELTINE (1947), 1933– , Cabinet Minister; as Minister of Defence (1985–6) involved in public quarrel with Sir John Cuckney (OS), Chairman of Westland.

PETER ROBERT LAMONT BROWN (1948), 1935– , Fellow of All Souls', Oxford; historian.

JOHN JEREMY KENRICK MOON (1948), 1934–74, 'One of the outstanding British painters of his generation.'

JAMES COLEMAN PFAUTZ (1948), 1930– , US Air Force General; attached to Pentagon, as Assistant Chief of Staff, Intelligence, 1983; Senior Military Fellow at Council on Foreign Relations, 1974; Distinguished Service Medal.

RICHARD REID INGRAMS (1950), 1937– , author, co-founder of *Private Eye*.

WILLIAM GEORGE RUSHTON (1950), 1937– , cartoonist, co-founder of *Private Eye*.

JOHN ROBERT PARKER RAVENSCROFT (1953), 1939– , under name of John Peel 'disc jockey', and writer on popular music.

MARTIN JOHN REES (1956), 1942– , FRS; Professor of Astronomy at Cambridge University since 1973; Heinemann Prize, 1984.

MICHAEL EDWIN PALIN (1957), 1943– , comedian, actor, writer.

CHRONOLOGY

February 10, 1552	The Royal Charter granted.
1561	Thomas Ashton becomes Headmaster
1564	Sir Philip Sidney and Sir Fulke Greville enter the school.
1578	Sealing of the Ordinances and death of Thomas Ashton.
1586	'The best attended school in England' (Camden).
1595–1630	Construction of the Old Schools.
ca1643	Loan to Charles I of £600.
1652	Judge Jeffreys enters the school.
1798	Act of Parliament repeals Ashton's Ordinances, and allows the rescue of the school. Samuel Butler becomes Headmaster.
Early 19th century	Origins of RSSH (The Hunt).
1818	Charles Darwin enters the school.
1836–1866	Headmastership of Benjamin Hall Kennedy.
1862	The Clarendon Commissioners visit the school.
1868	Shrewsbury included as one of seven schools in the Public Schools Act.
1882	The move to Kingsland.
1908–1916	Headmastership of Cyril Alington.
1939–1940	Cheltenham 'billeted' at Shrewsbury for two terms.
1963–1975	Headmastership of Donald Wright; construction of Kingsland Hall (1968–69).

INDEX

This is a brief and selective index, aiming at utility rather than completeness; it omits (for example) the names of those Salopians who otherwise appear only in the list which runs from pages 137 to 142, but gives at least some references to matters of interest, the existence or location of which could not be speedily inferred from the *Contents* (p. vii). It impartially includes the names of persons, places and books, as well as some subject headings (e.g. social, academic, and sporting). Some early Headmasters will be found only in the list given on p. 135. Following this index, there is a separate one for the illustrations.

INDEX TO ILLUSTRATIONS